World Children's Day

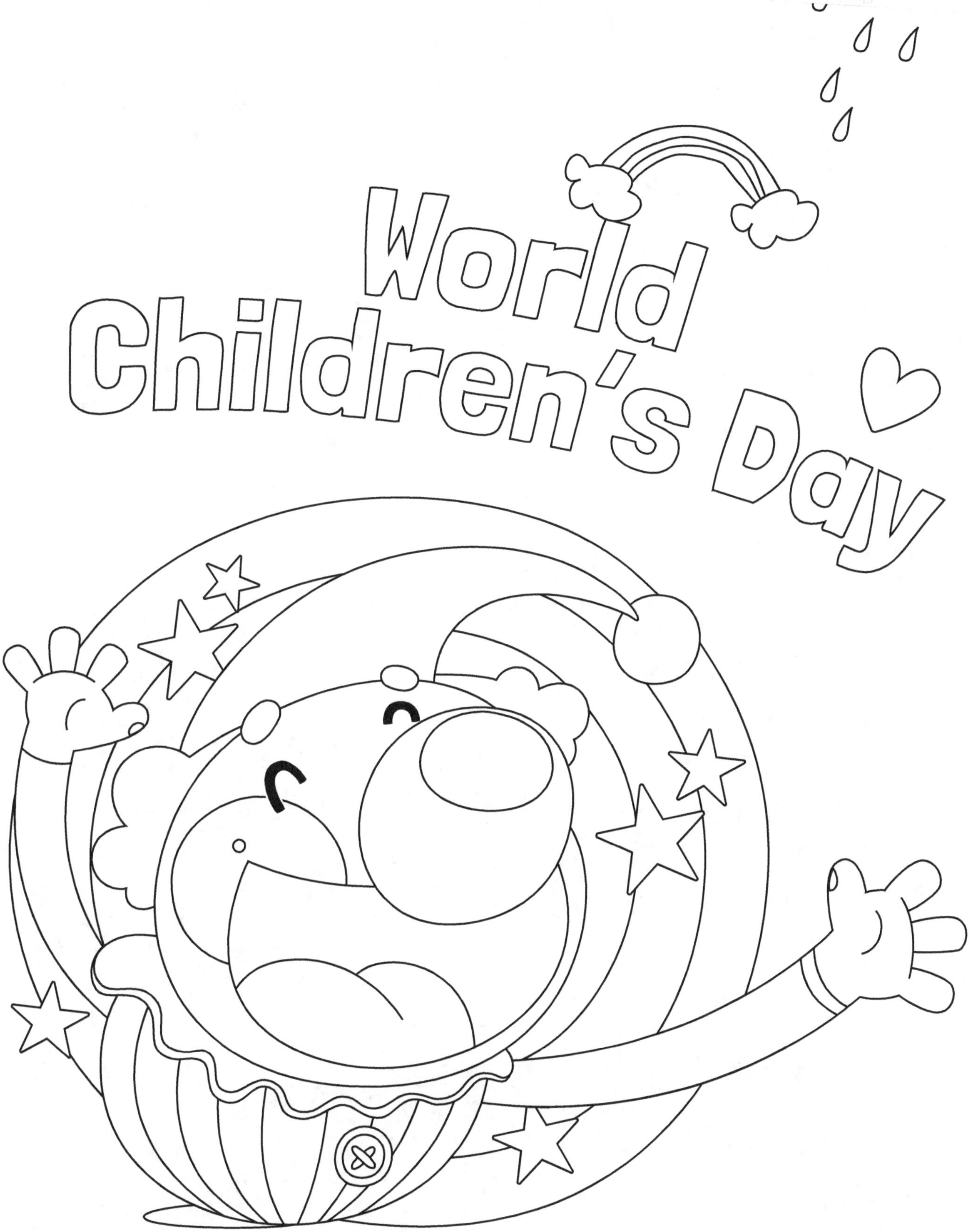

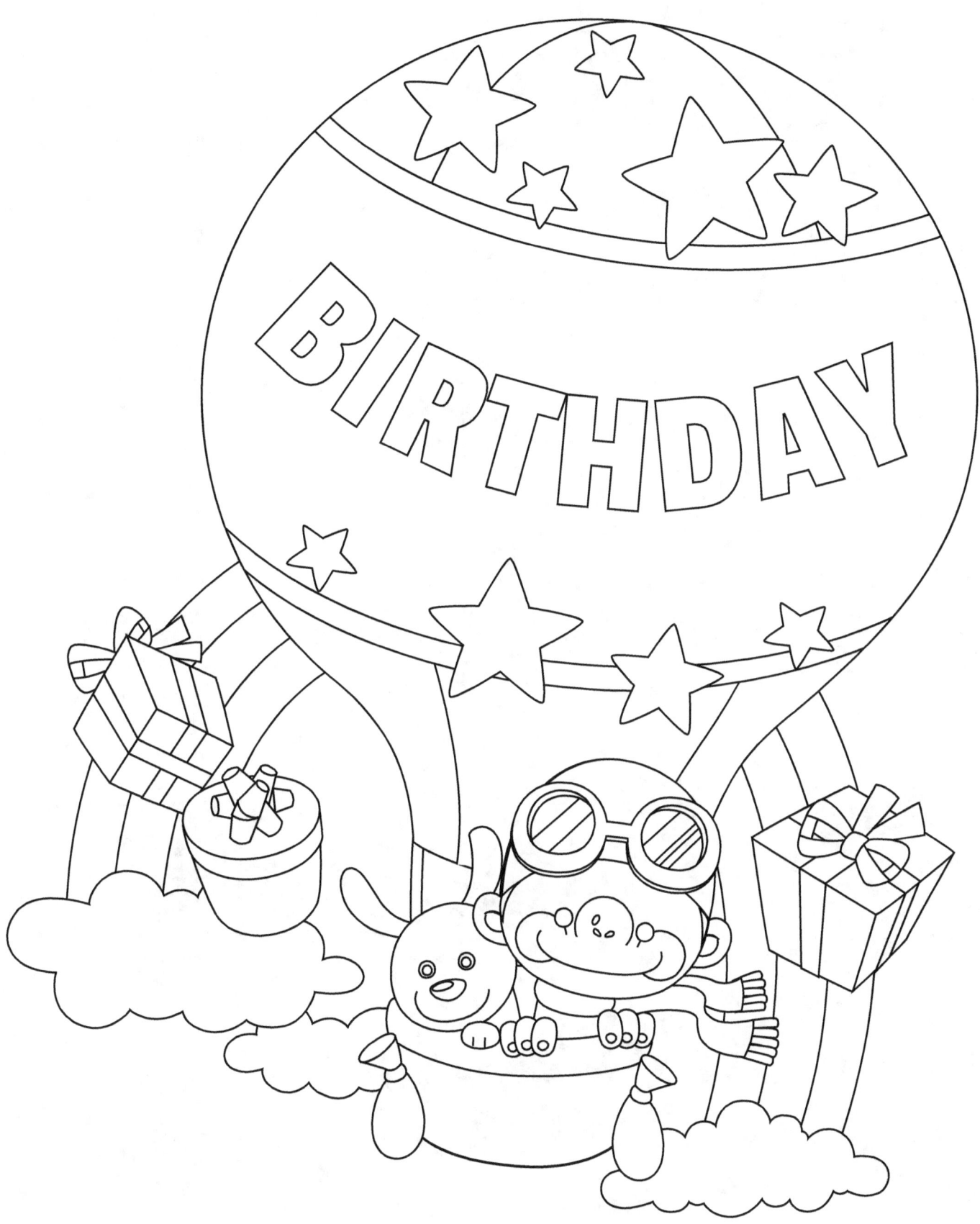

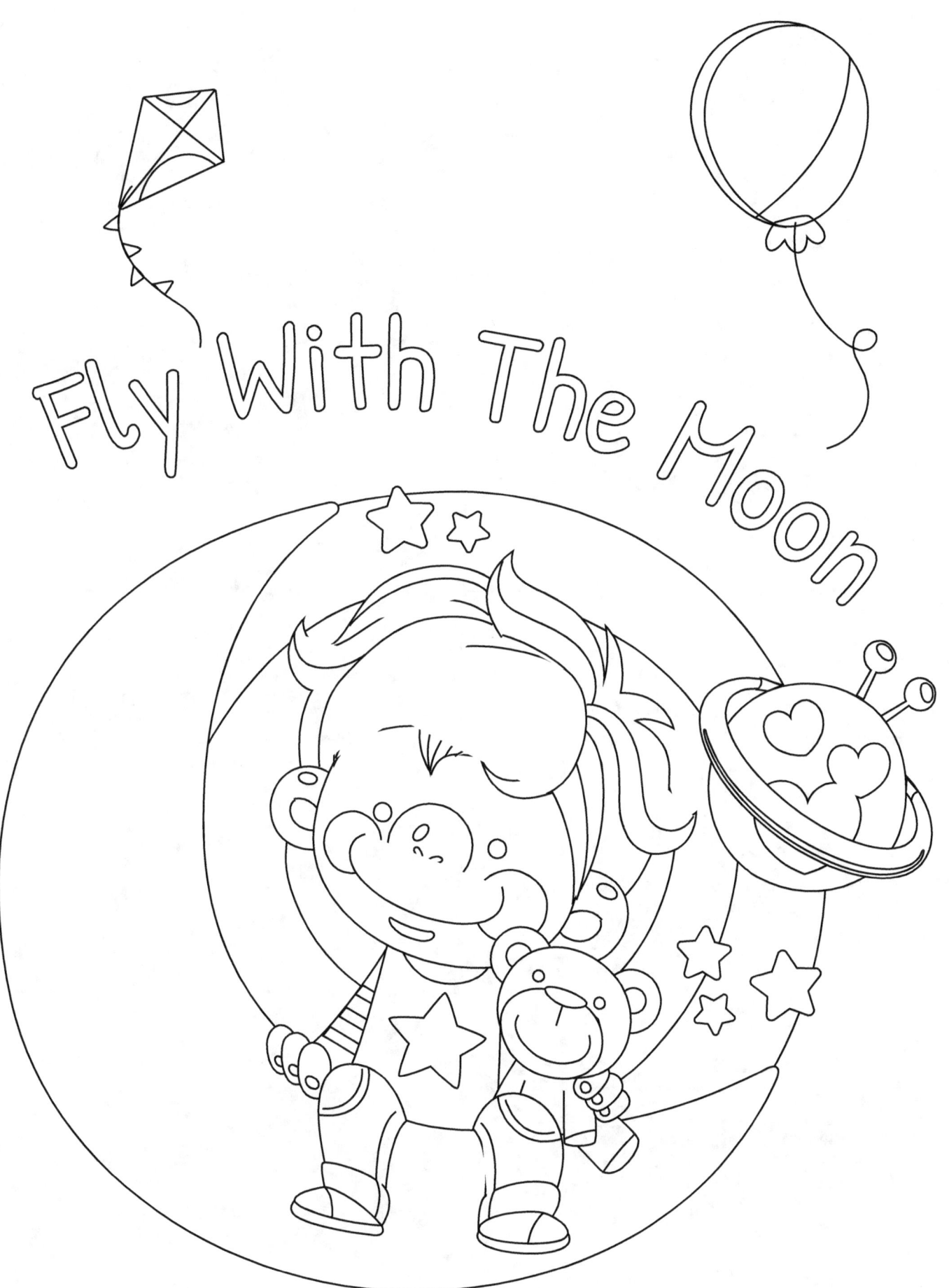

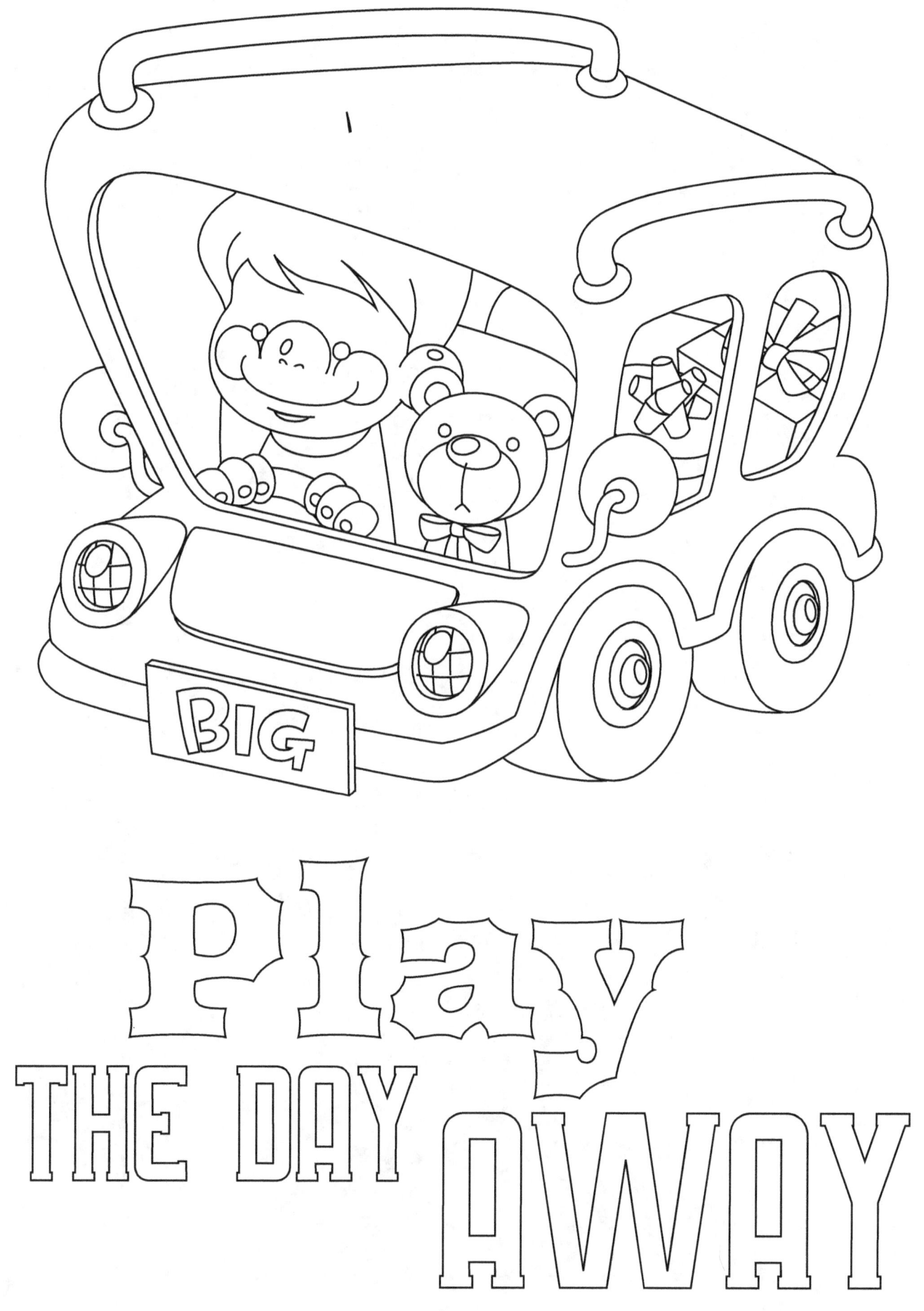

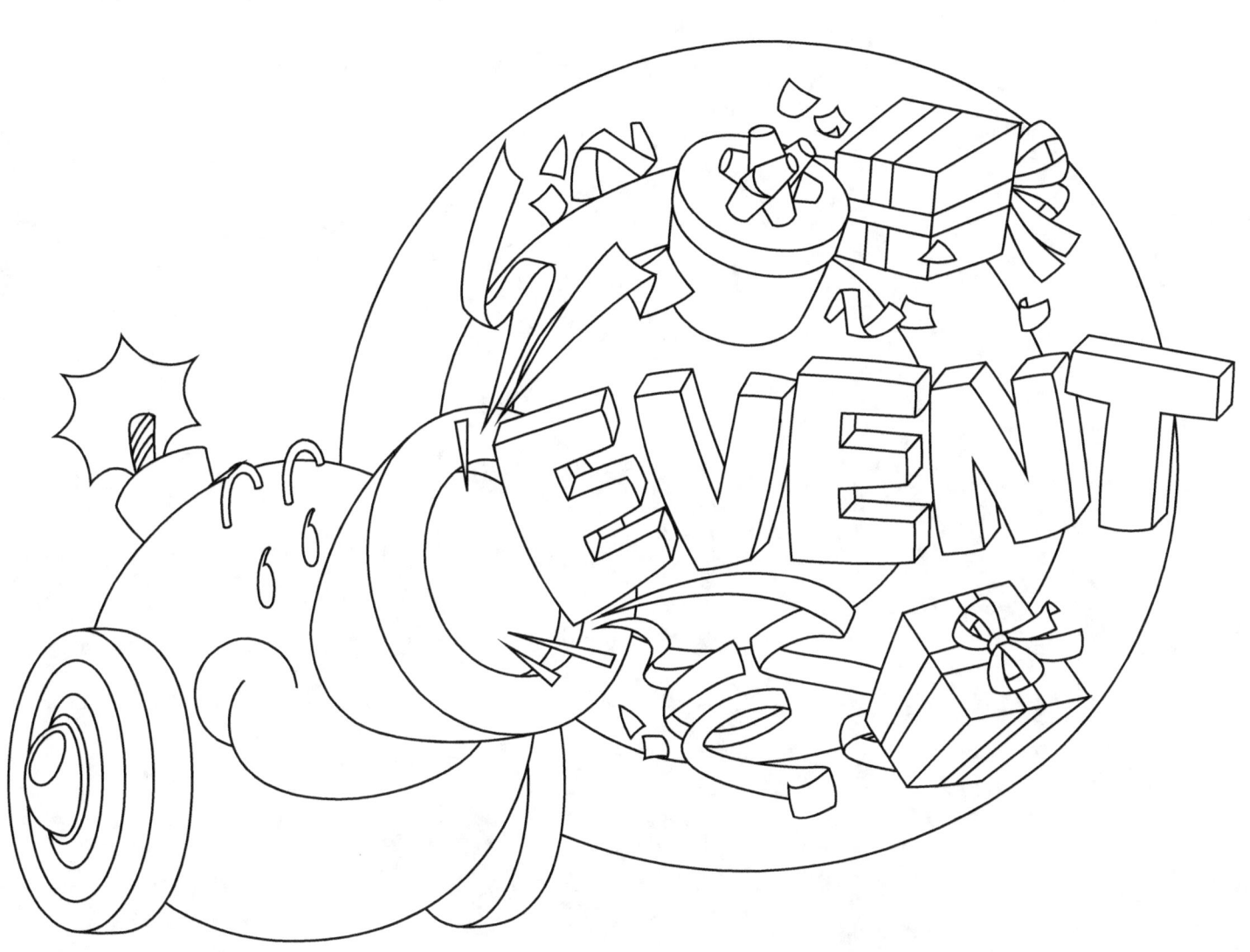

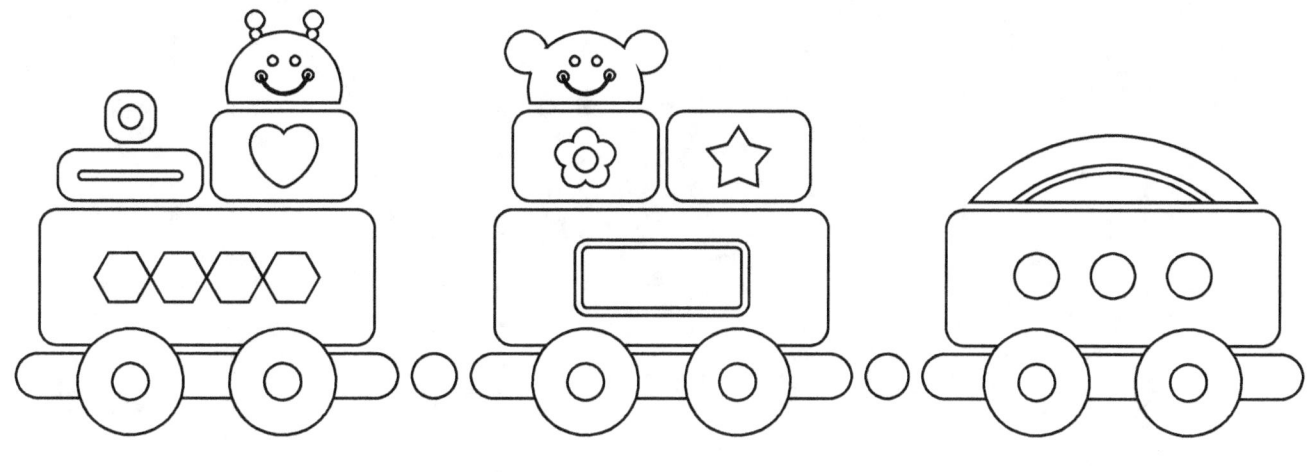

Technical Designer

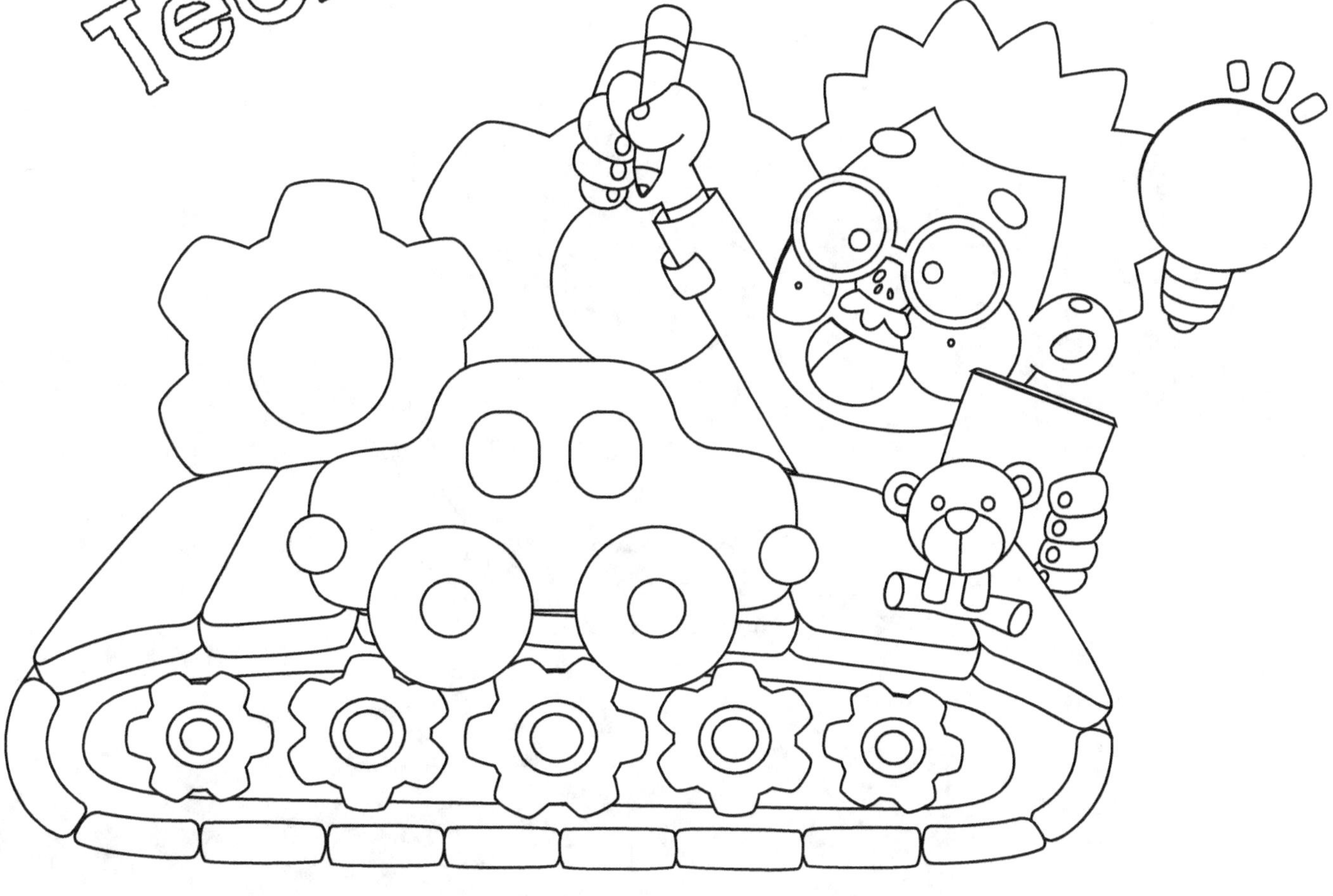

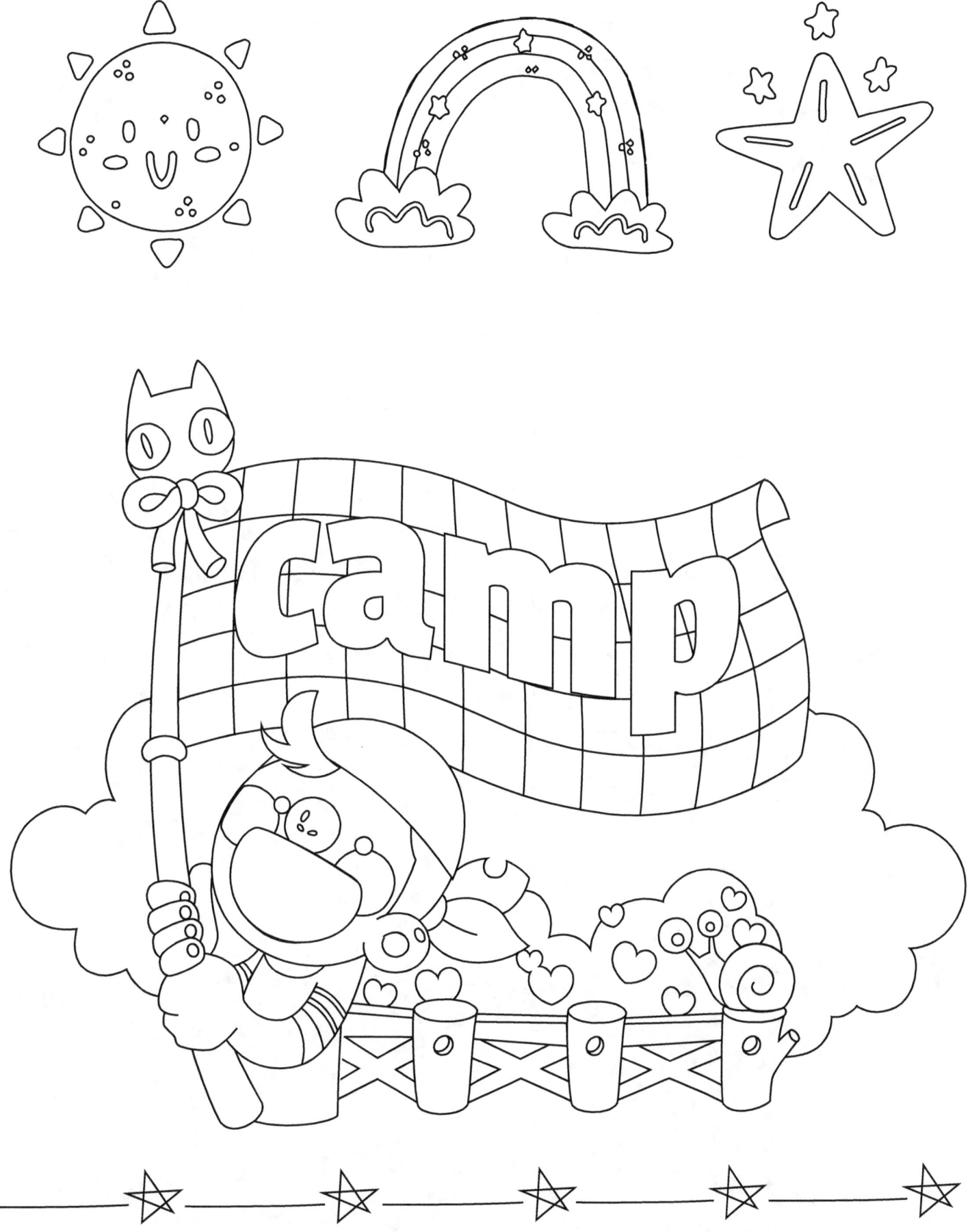

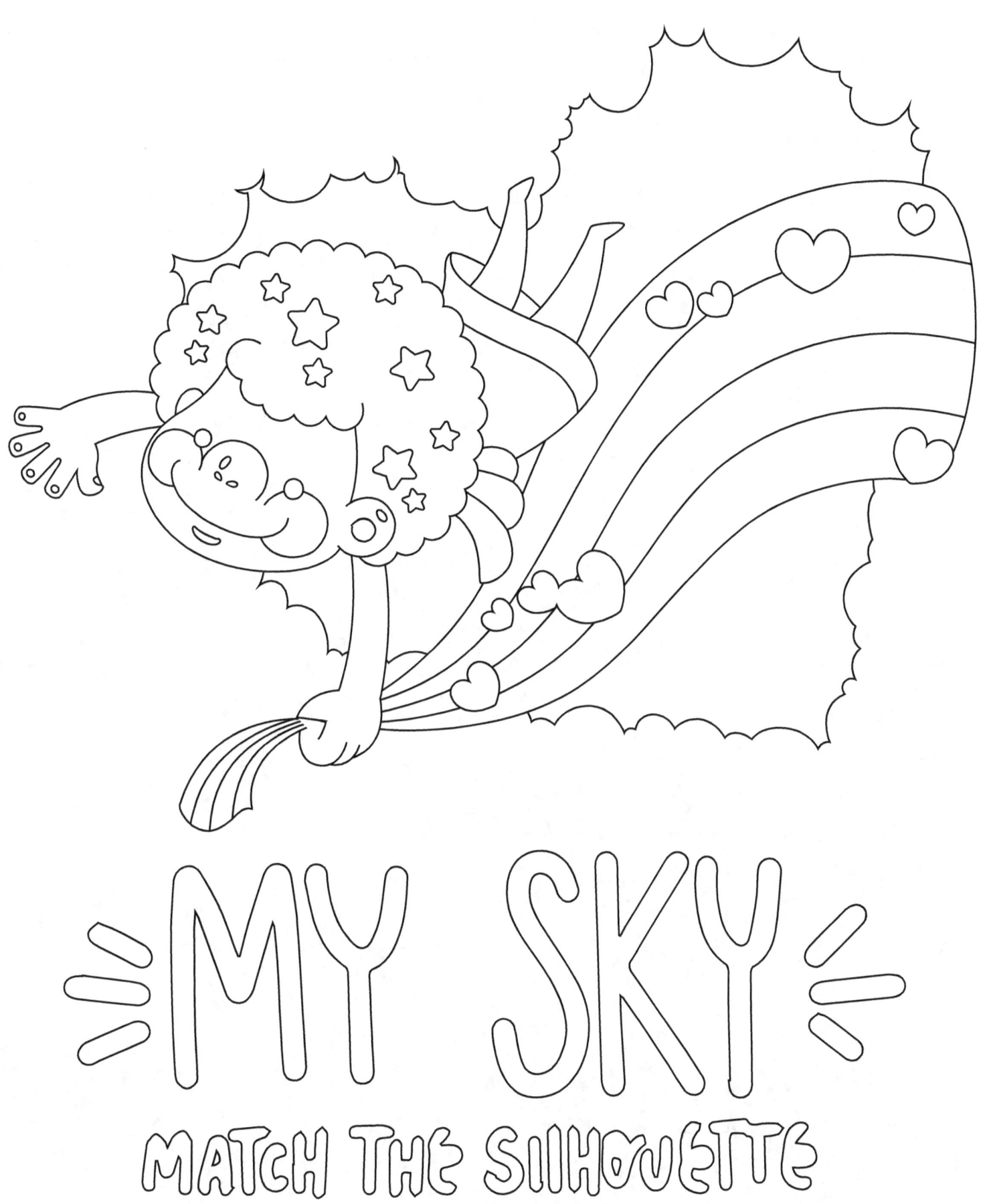

MY SKY

MATCH THE SILHOUETTE

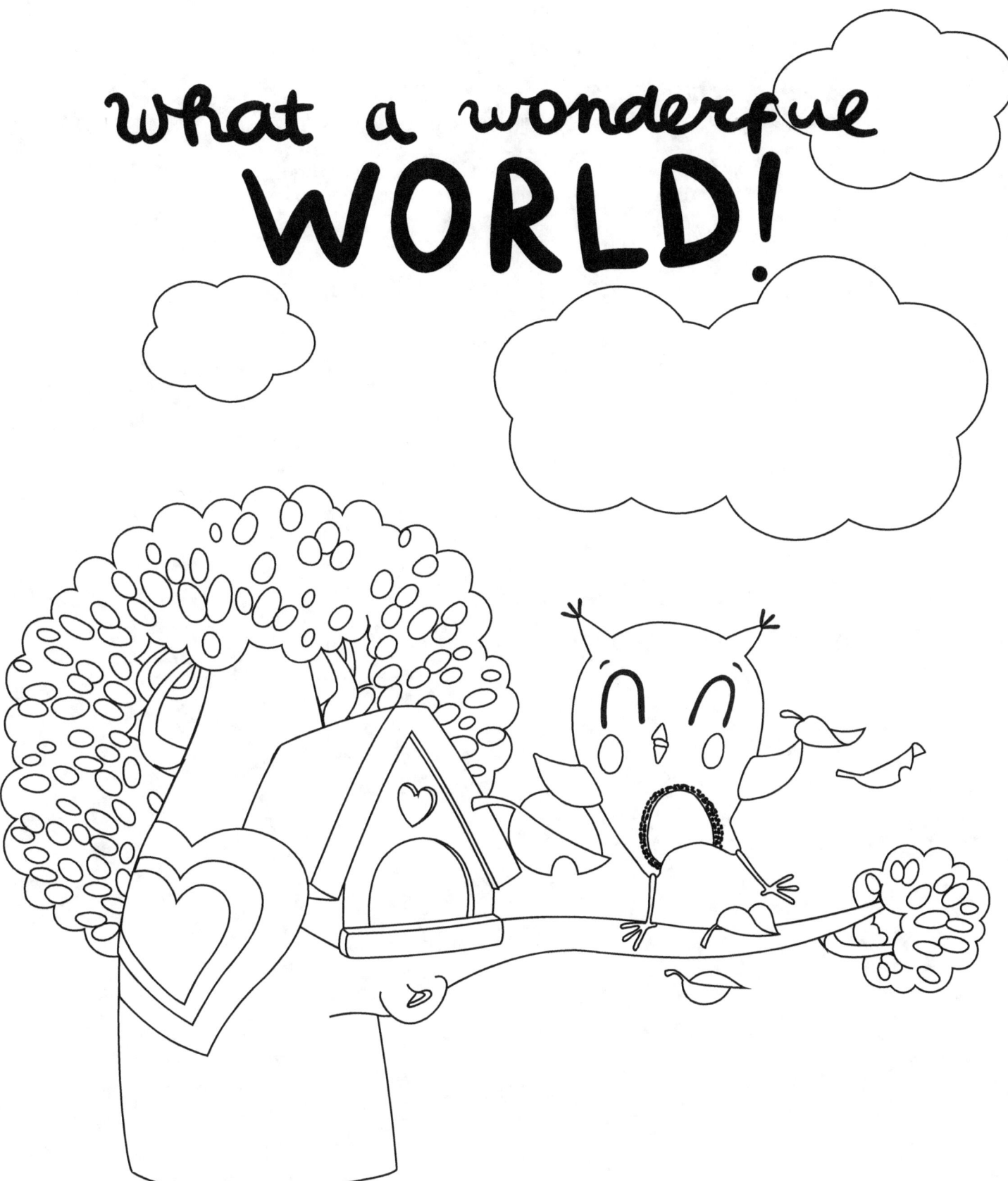

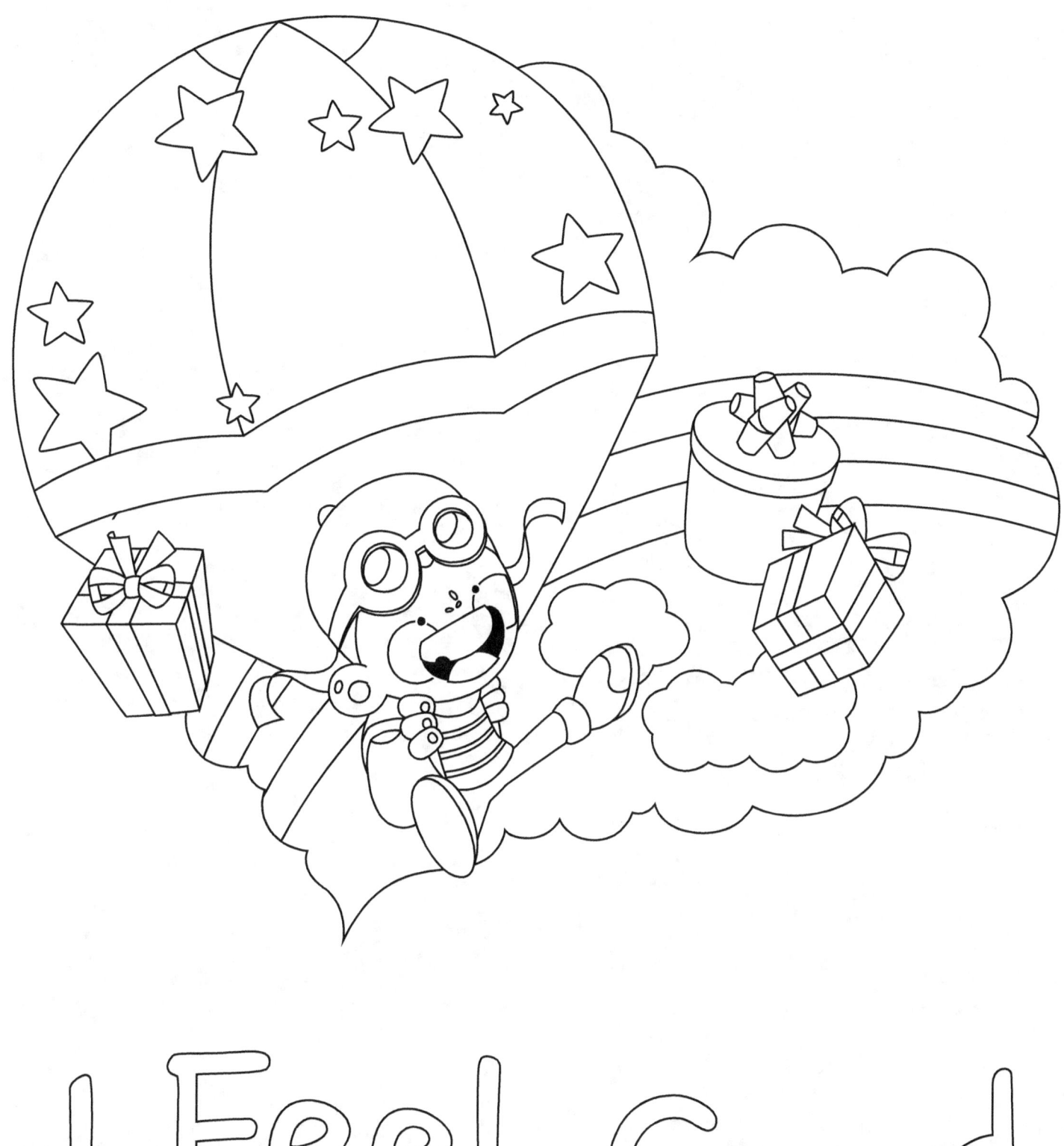

I Feel Good

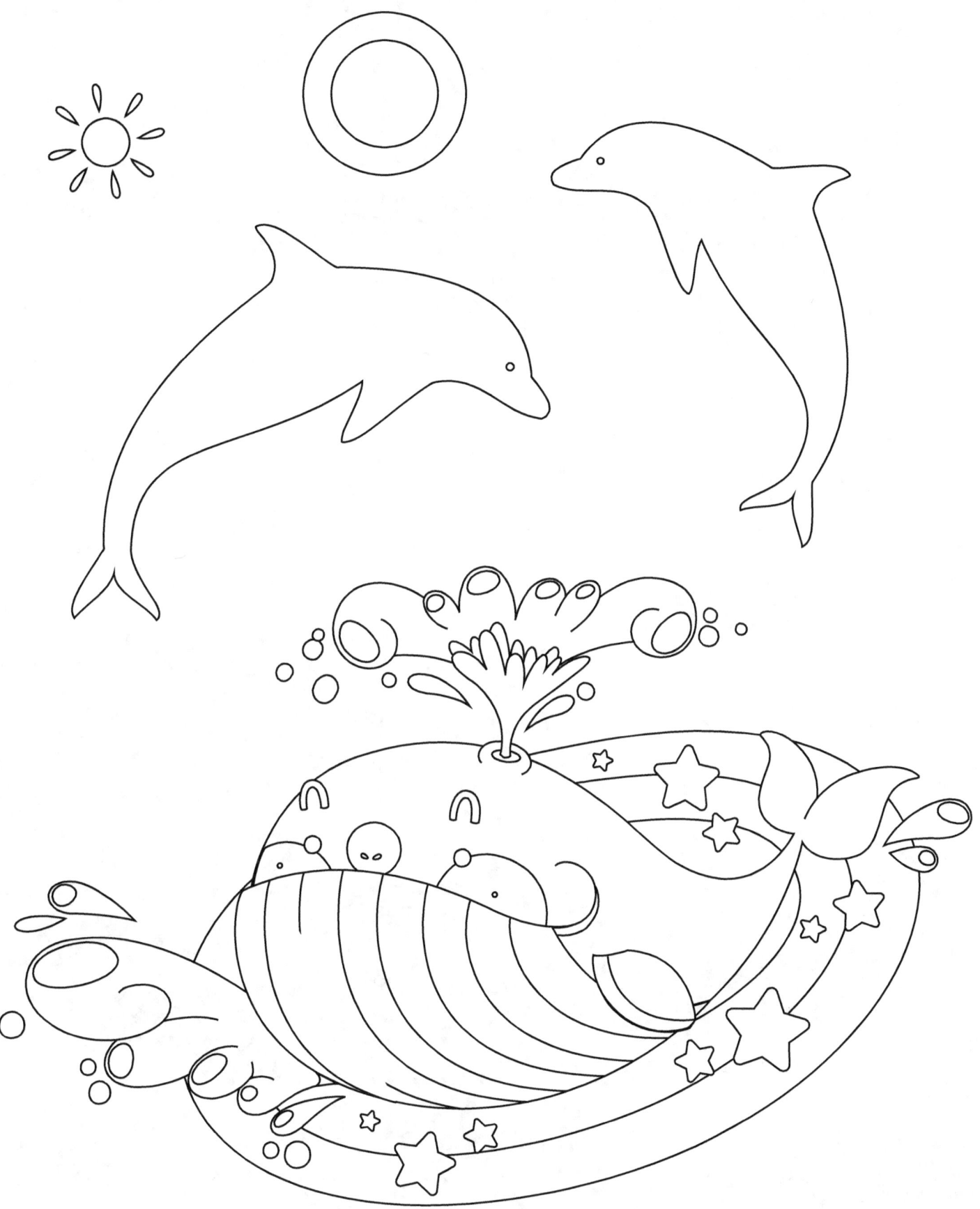

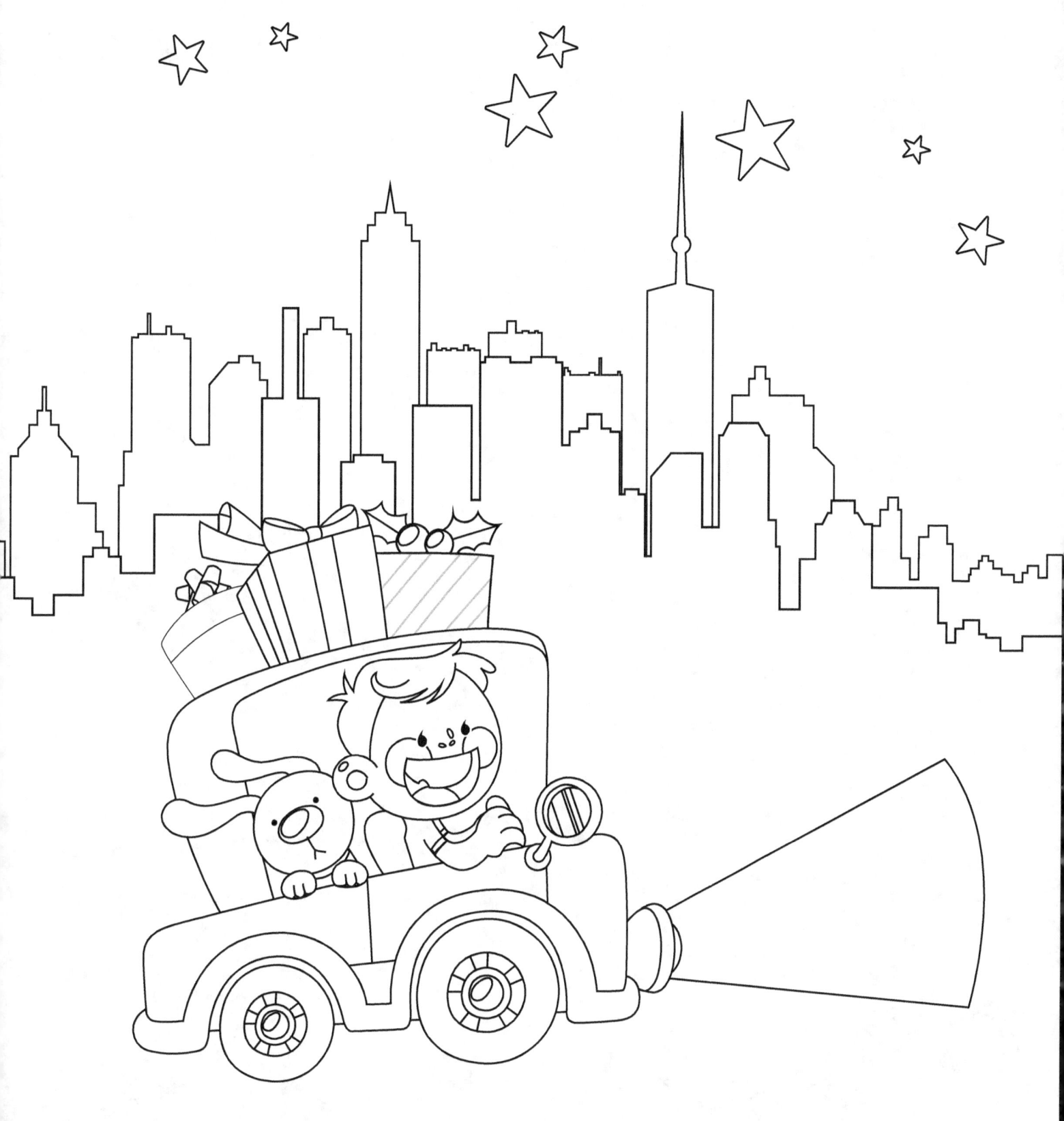

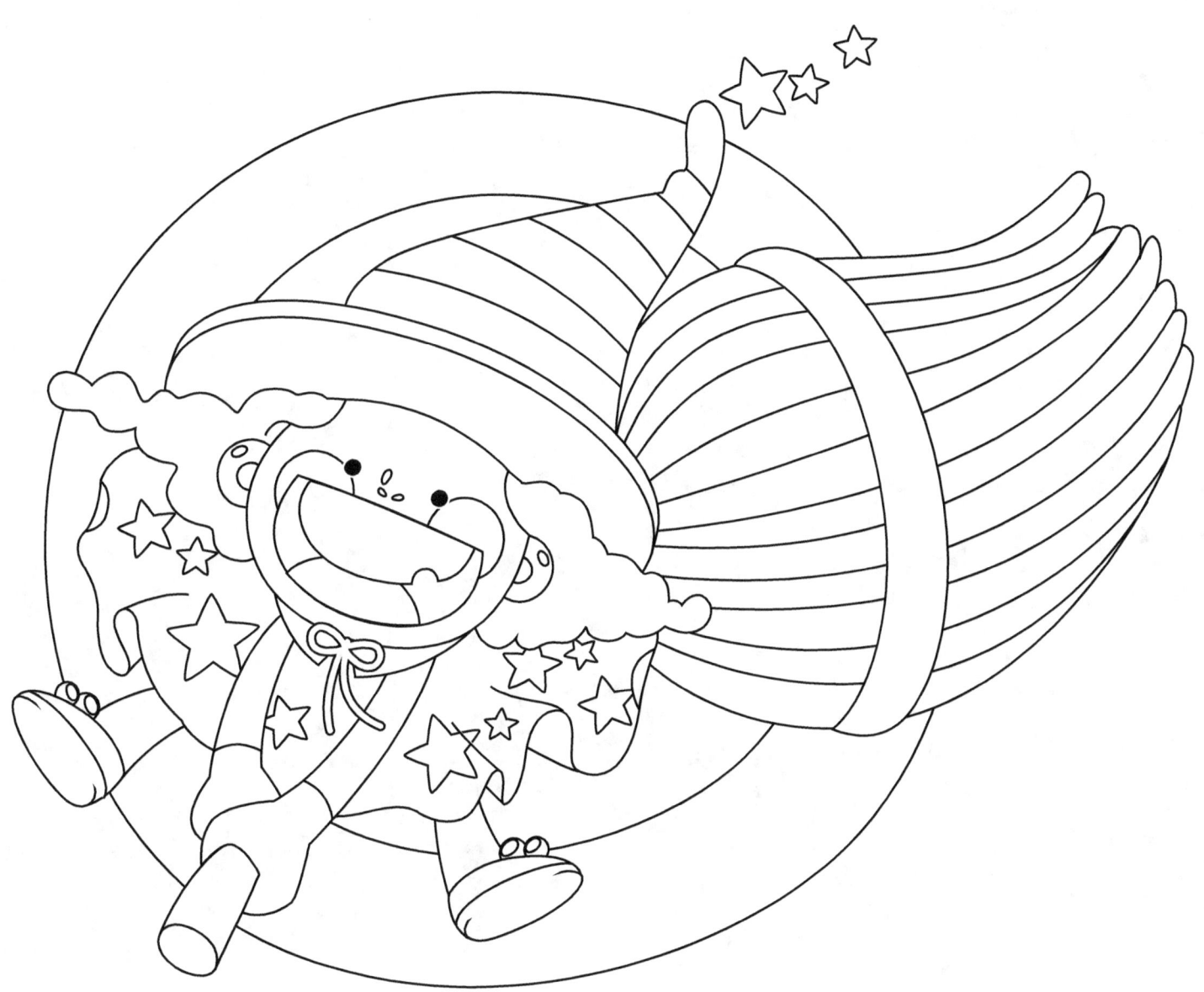

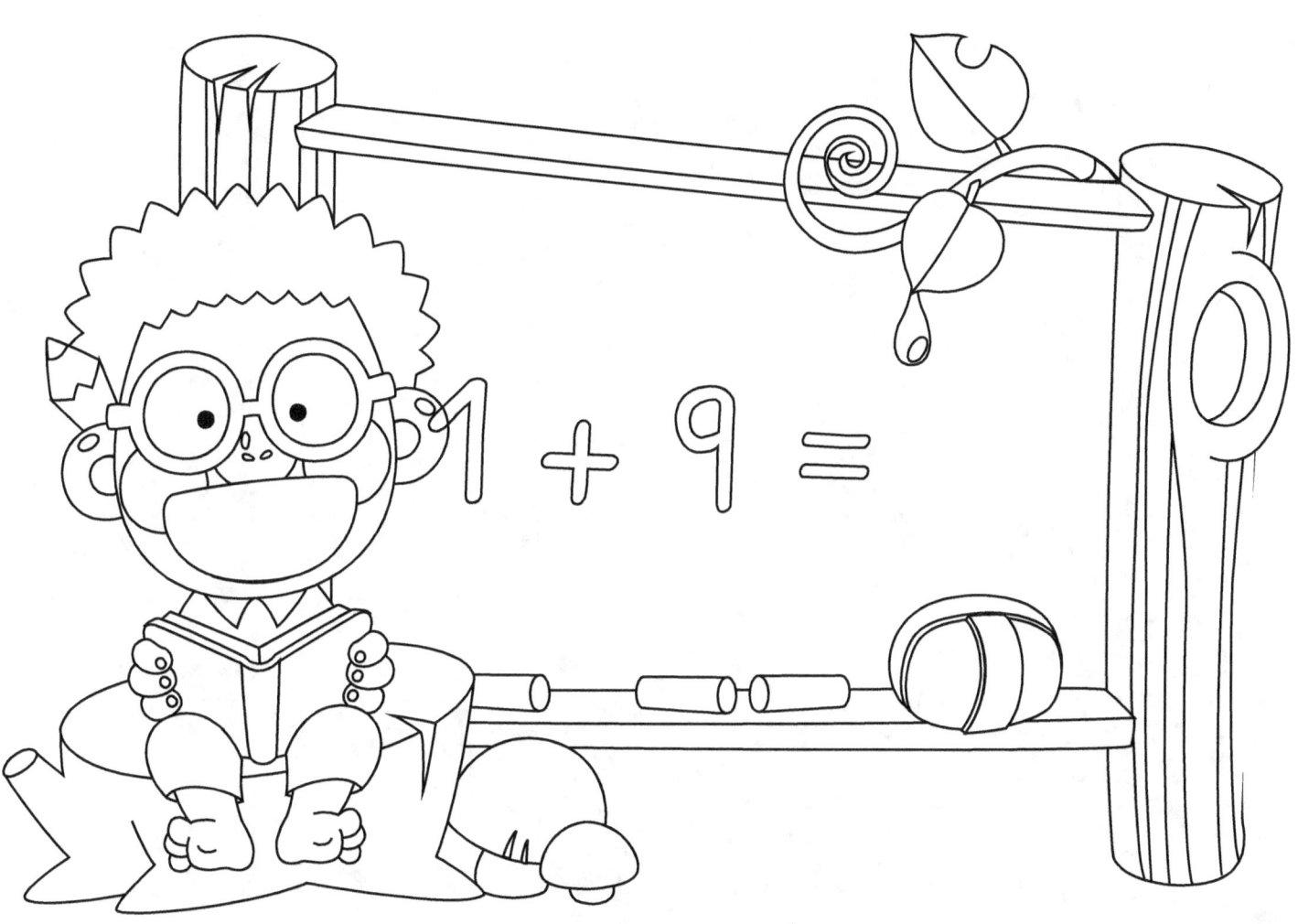

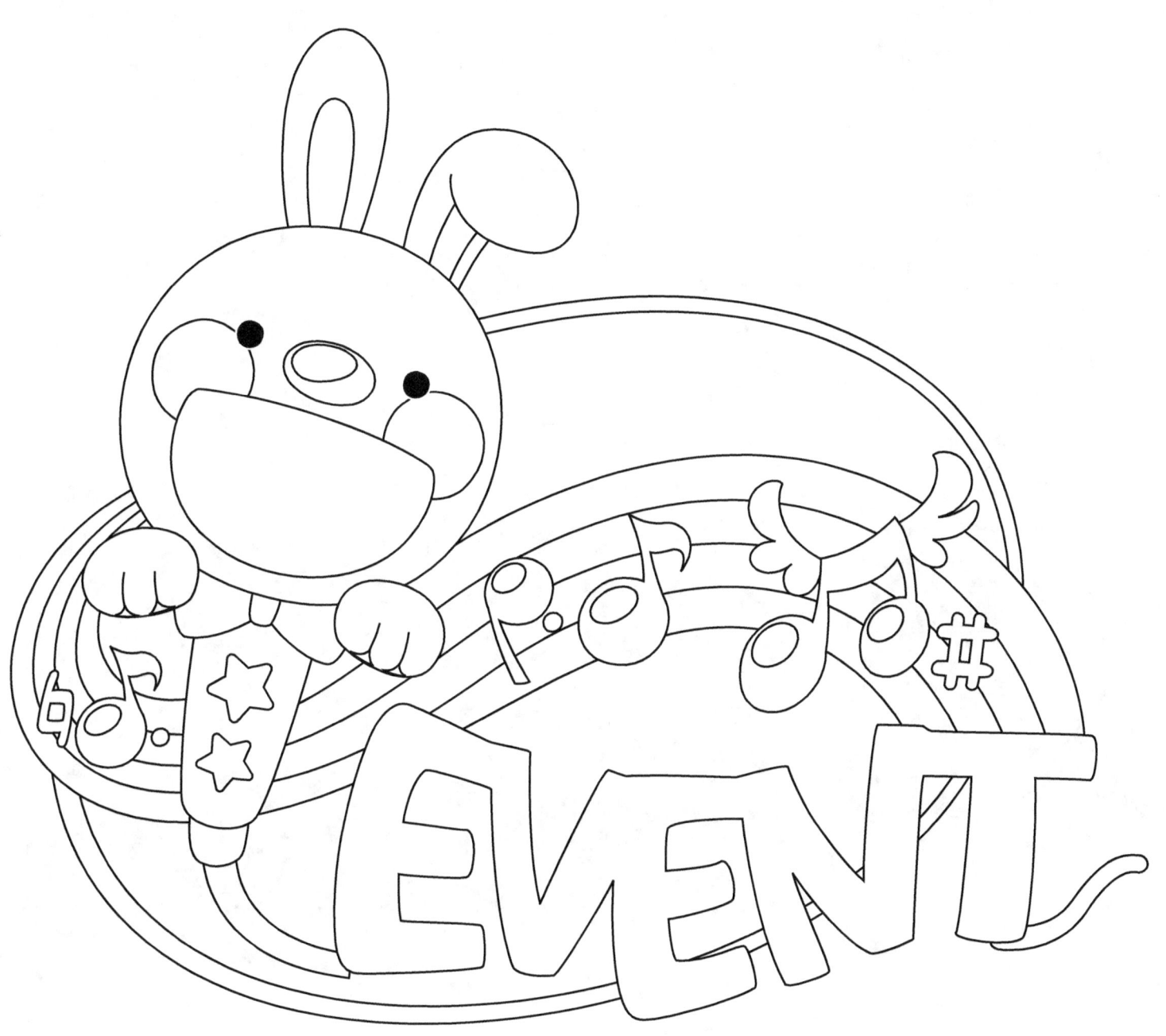

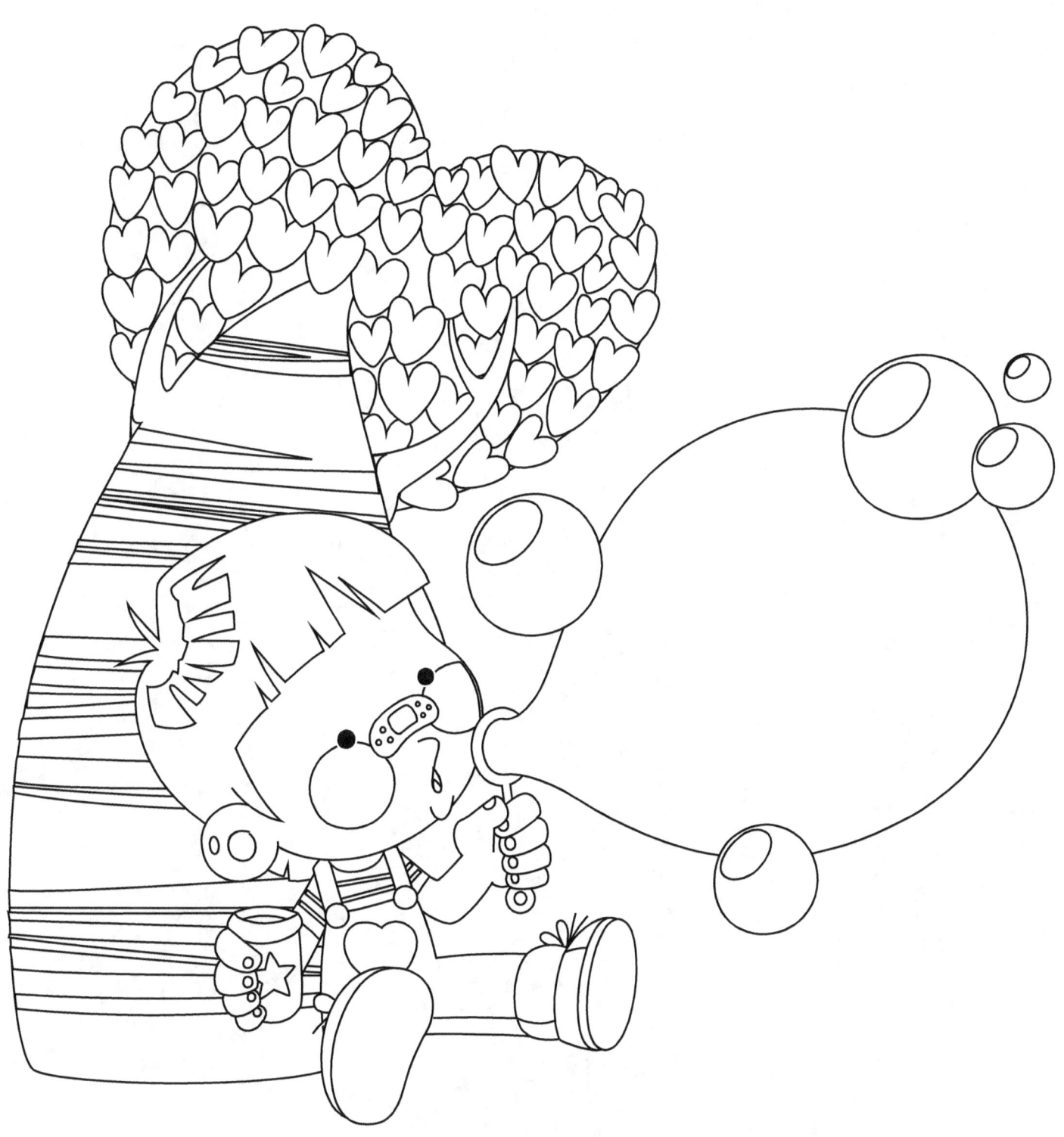

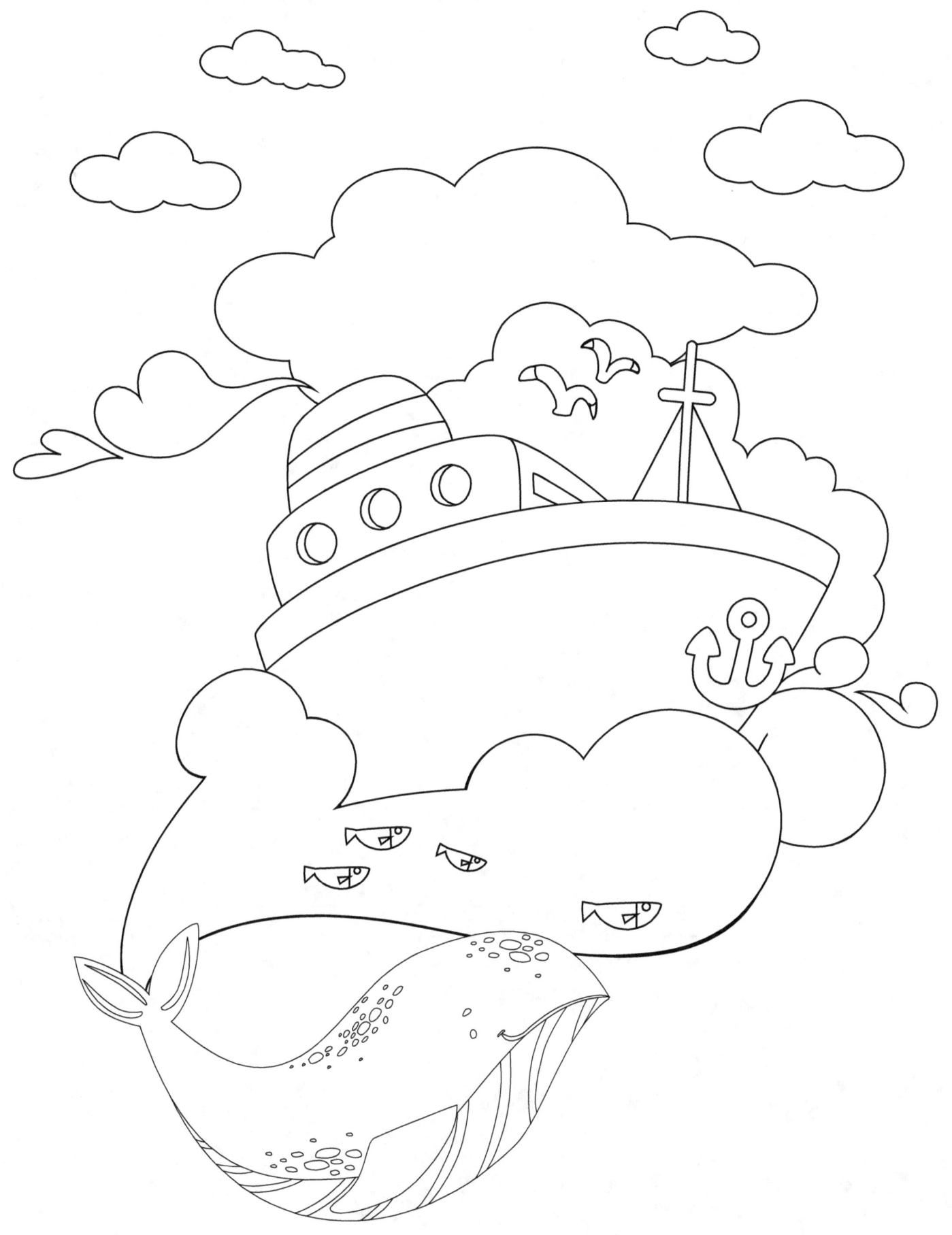

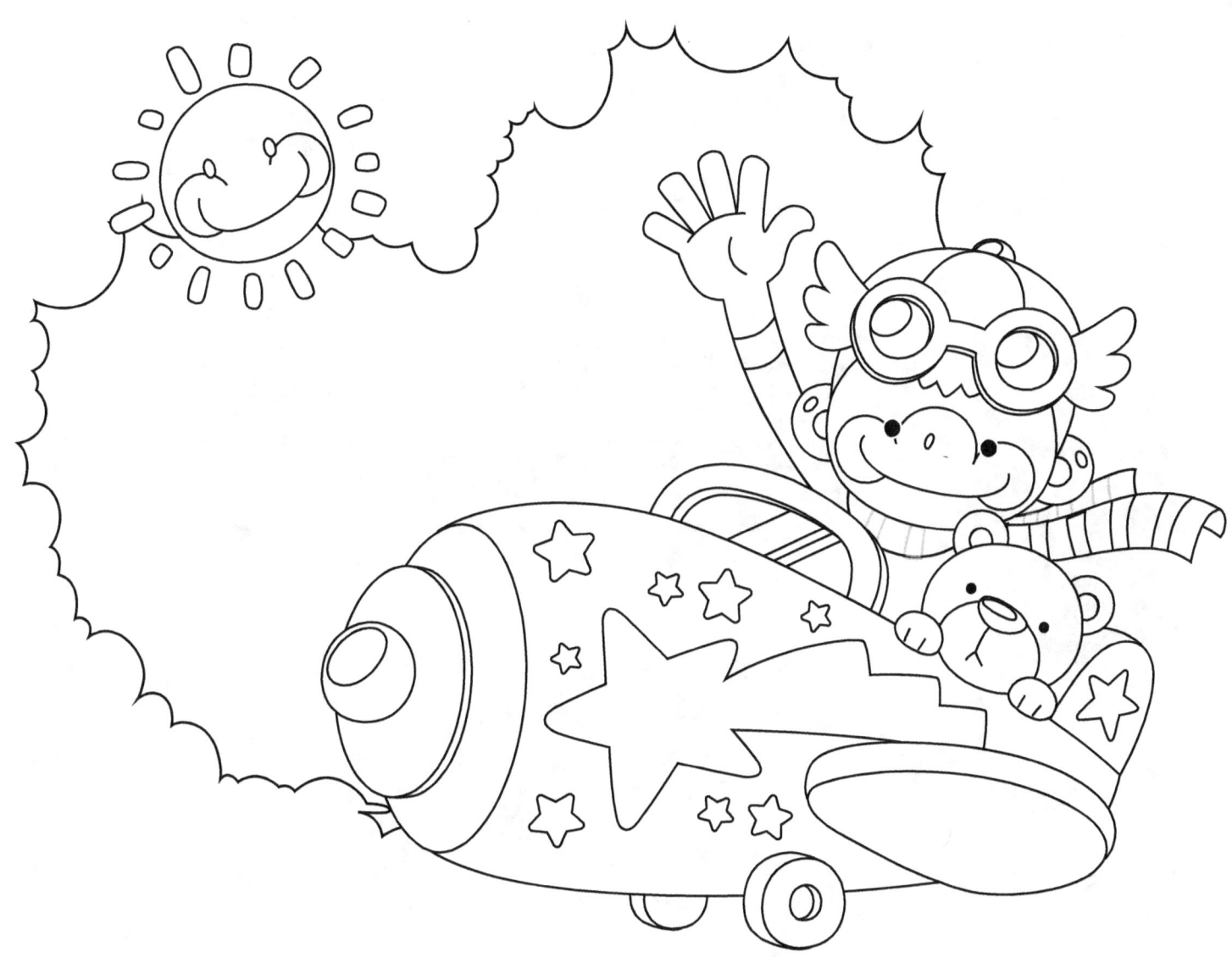

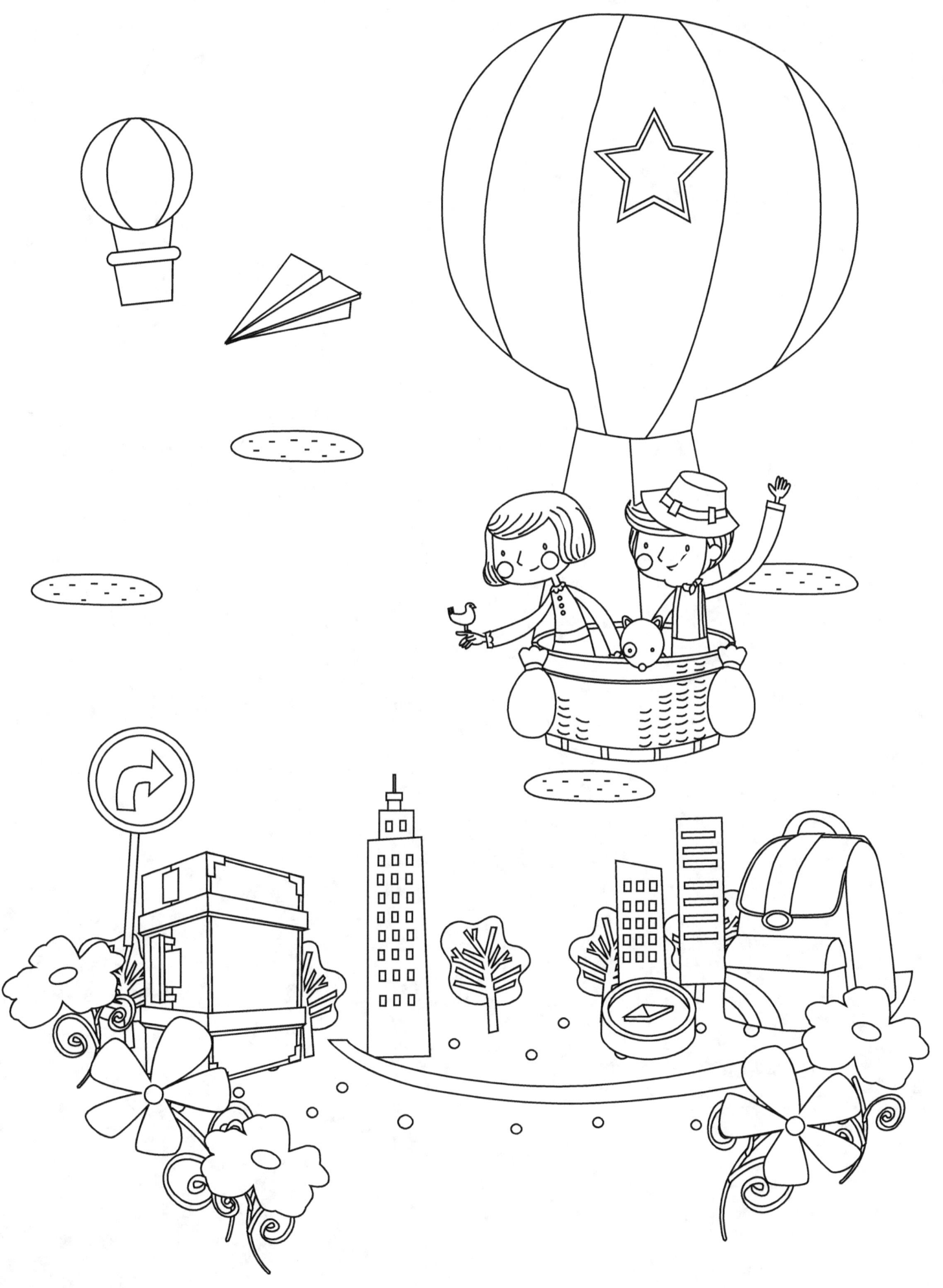

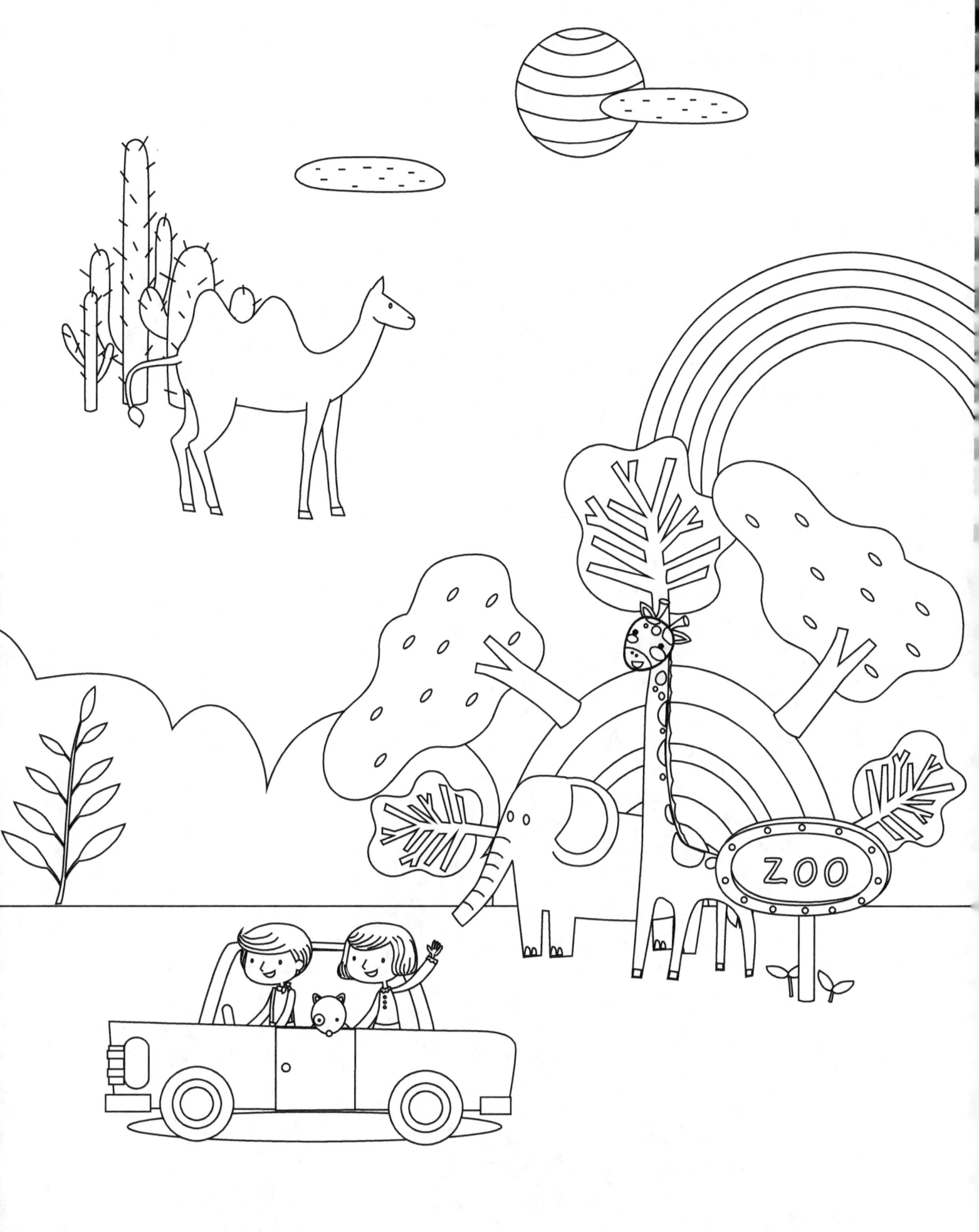

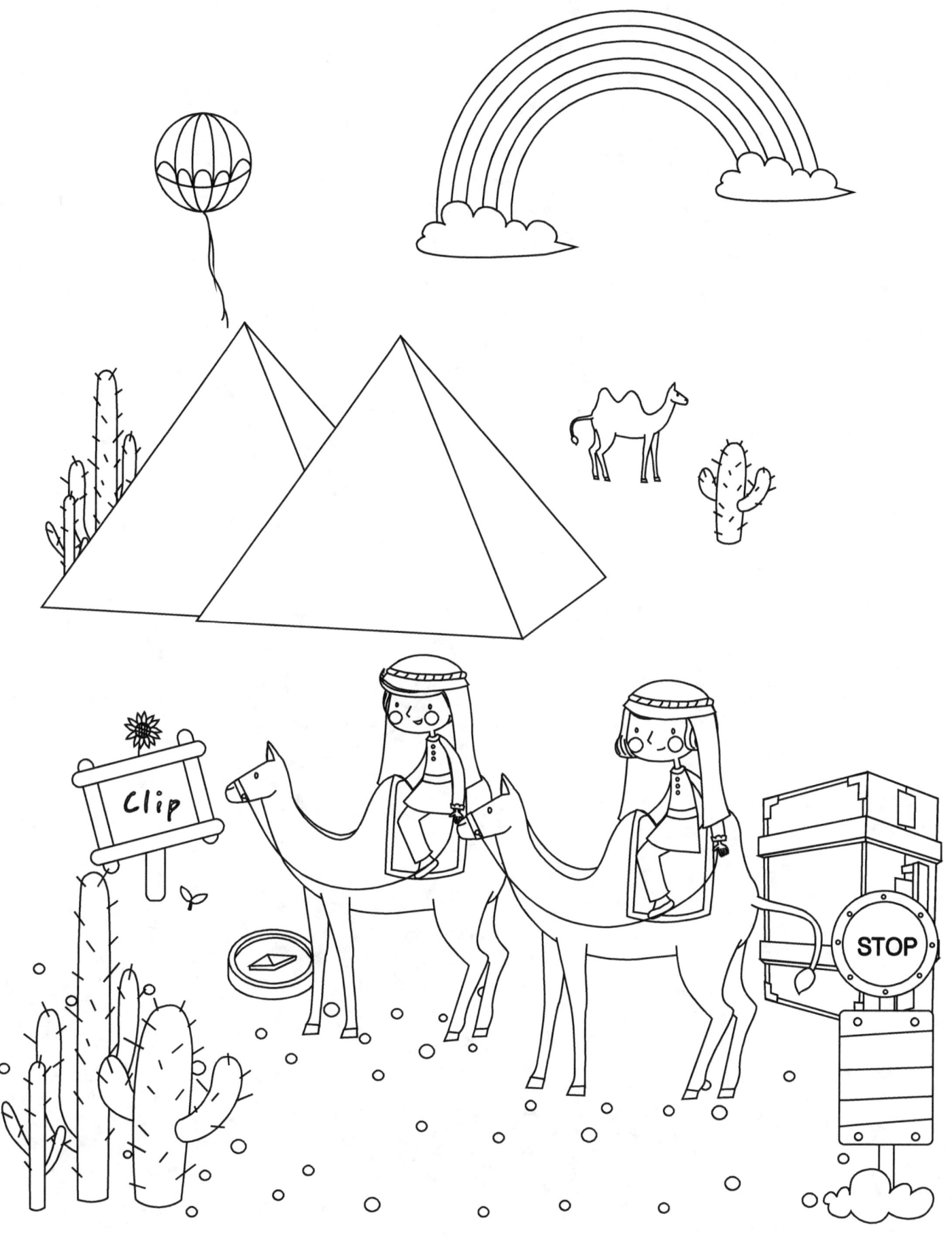

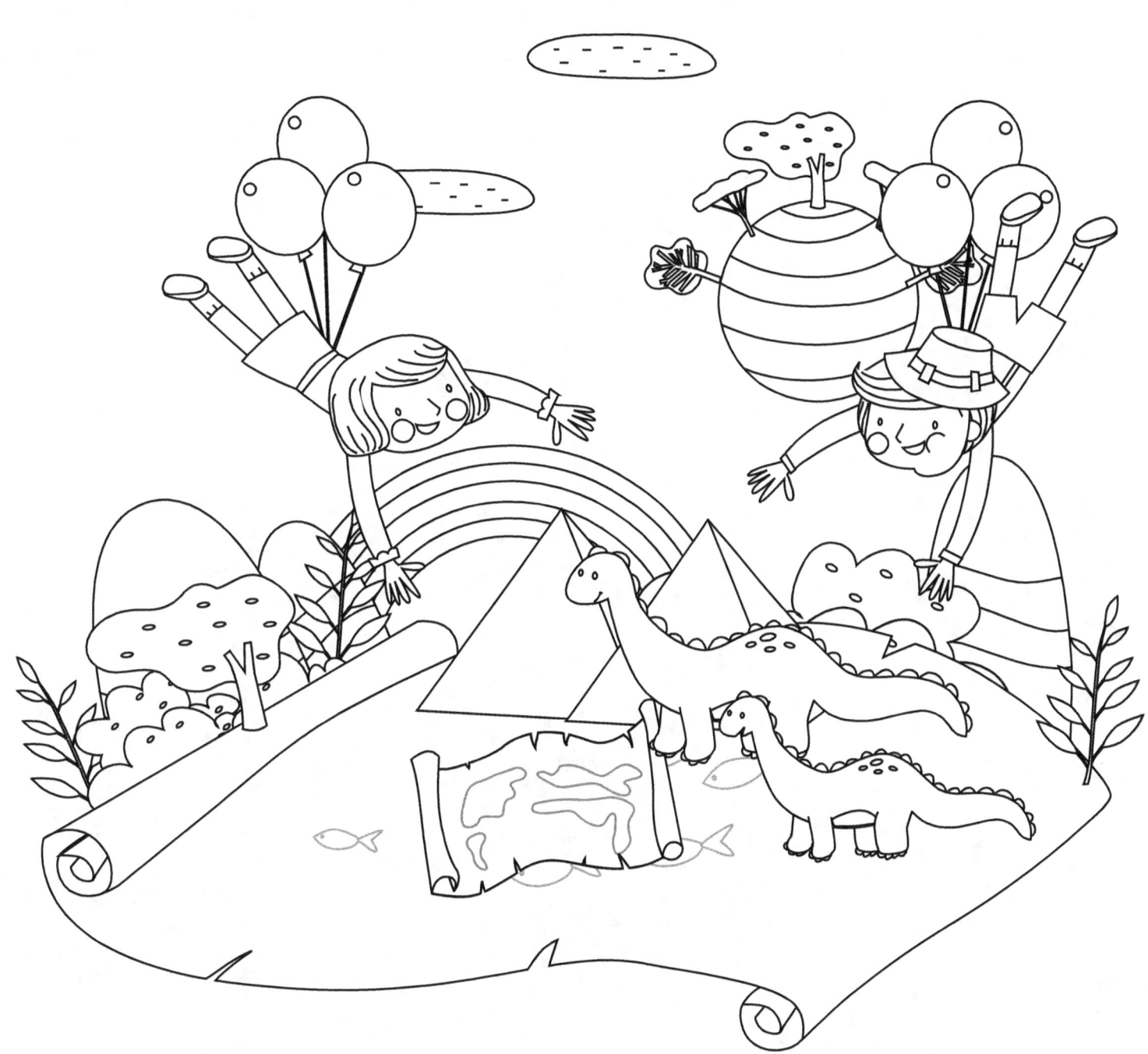

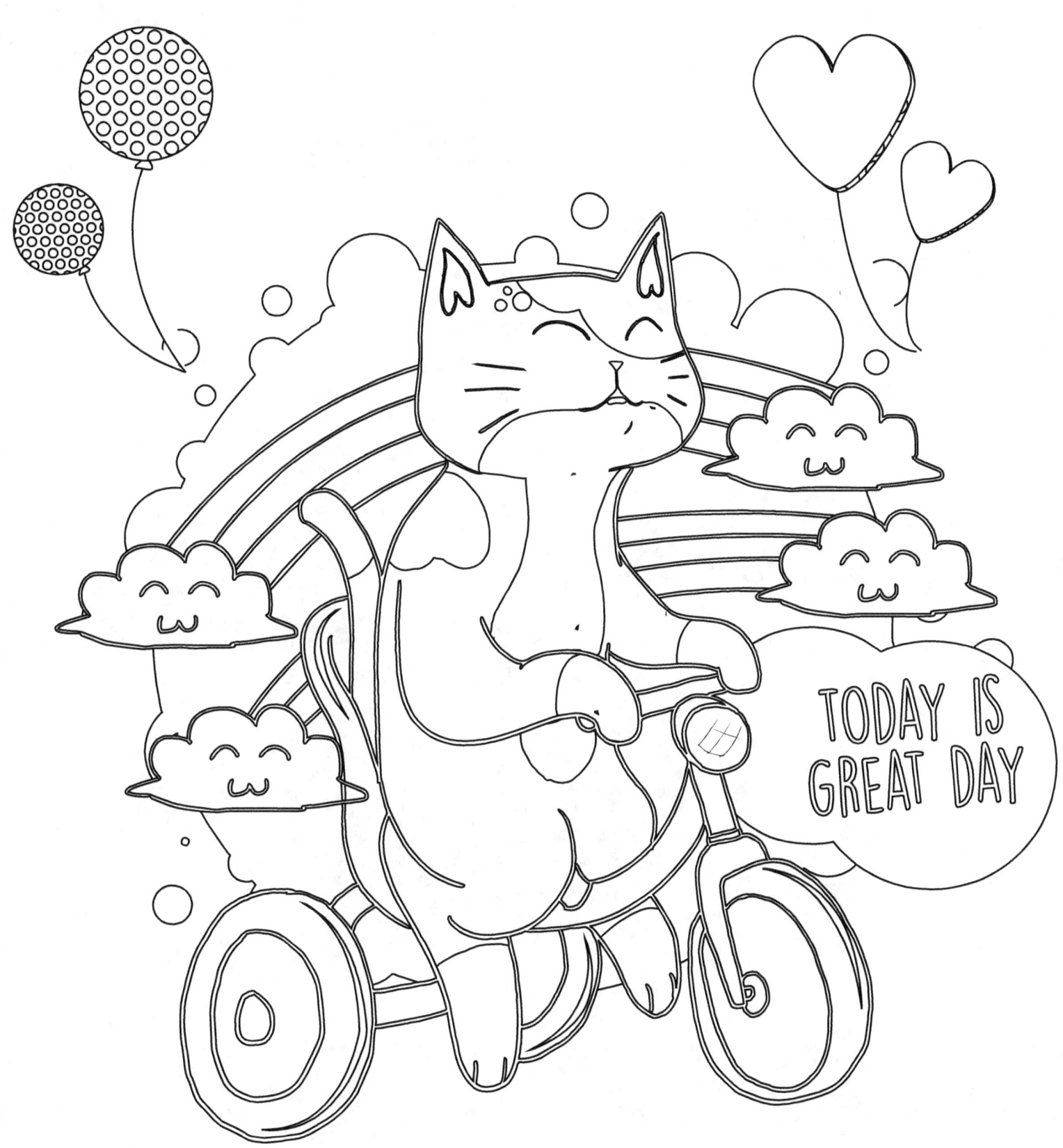

SWEET dreams LITTLE ONE

playing with me !

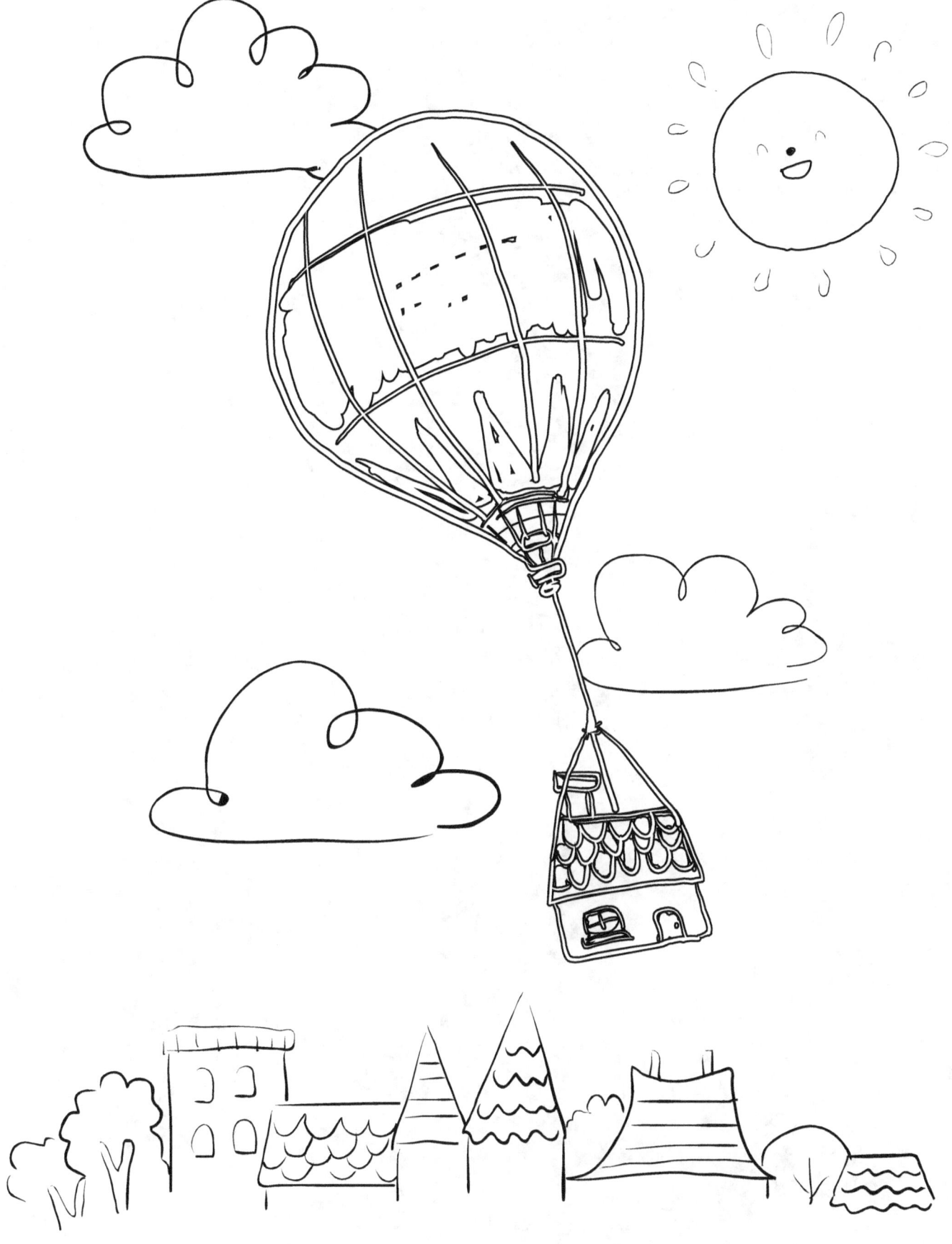

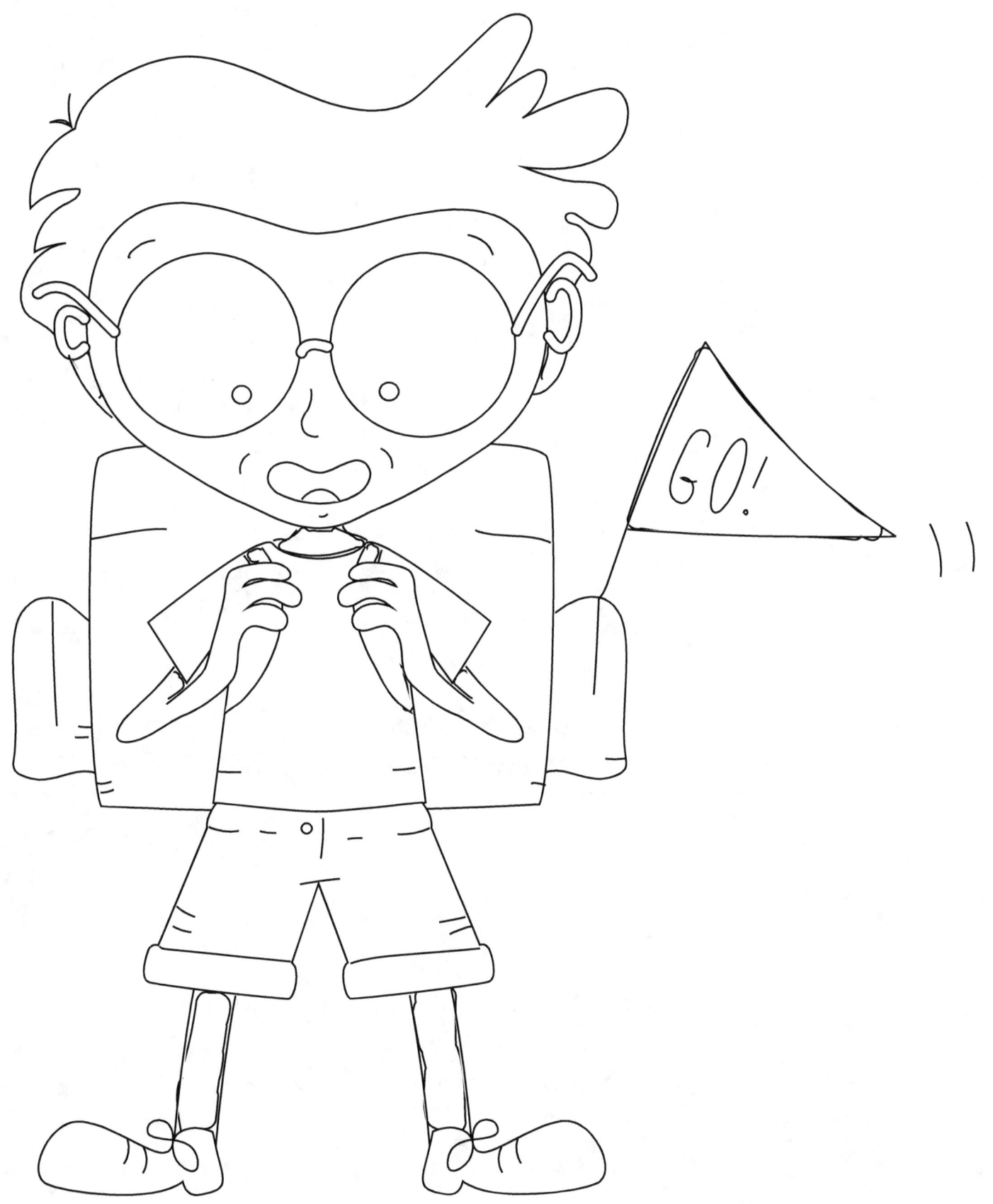

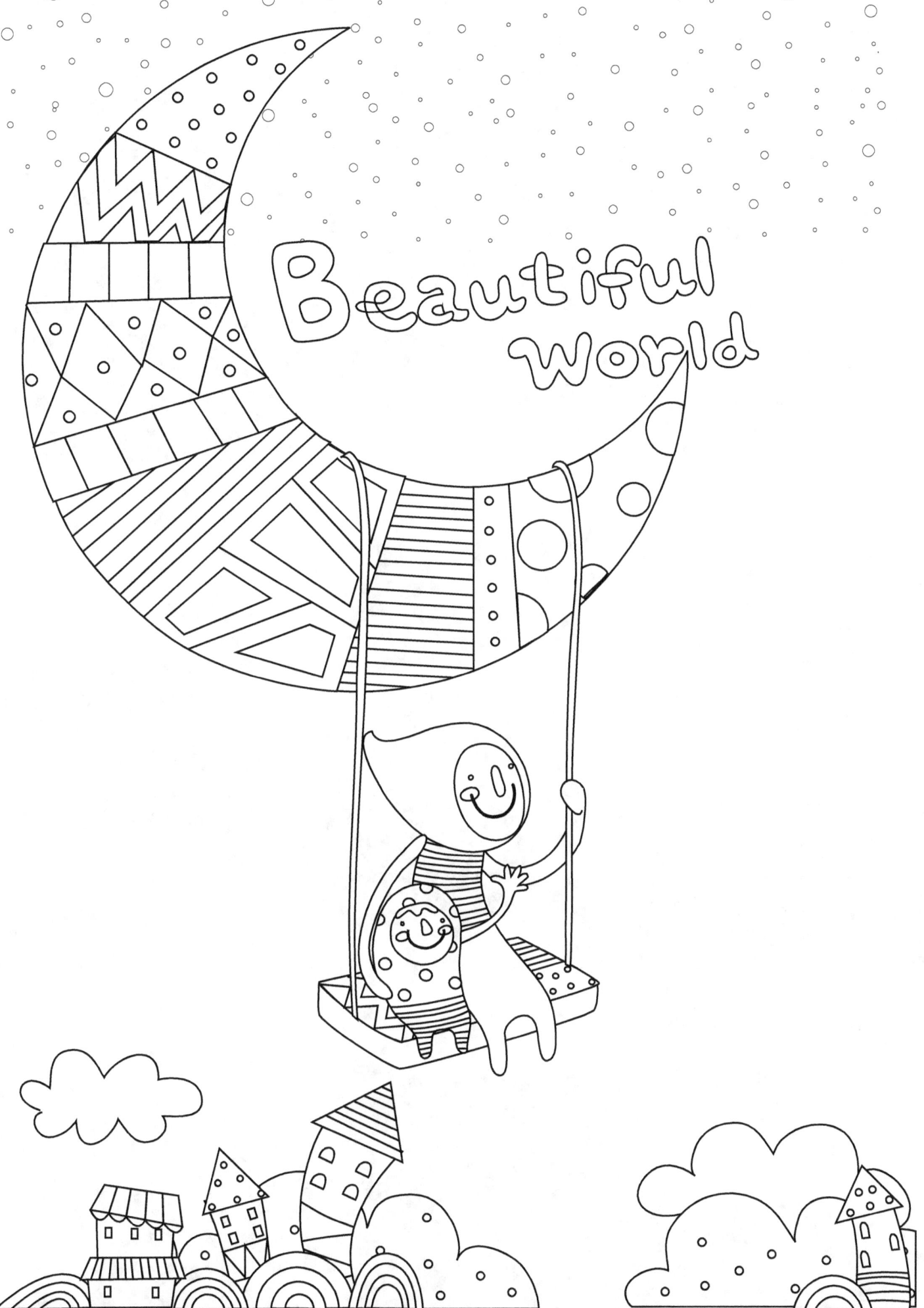

Beautiful World

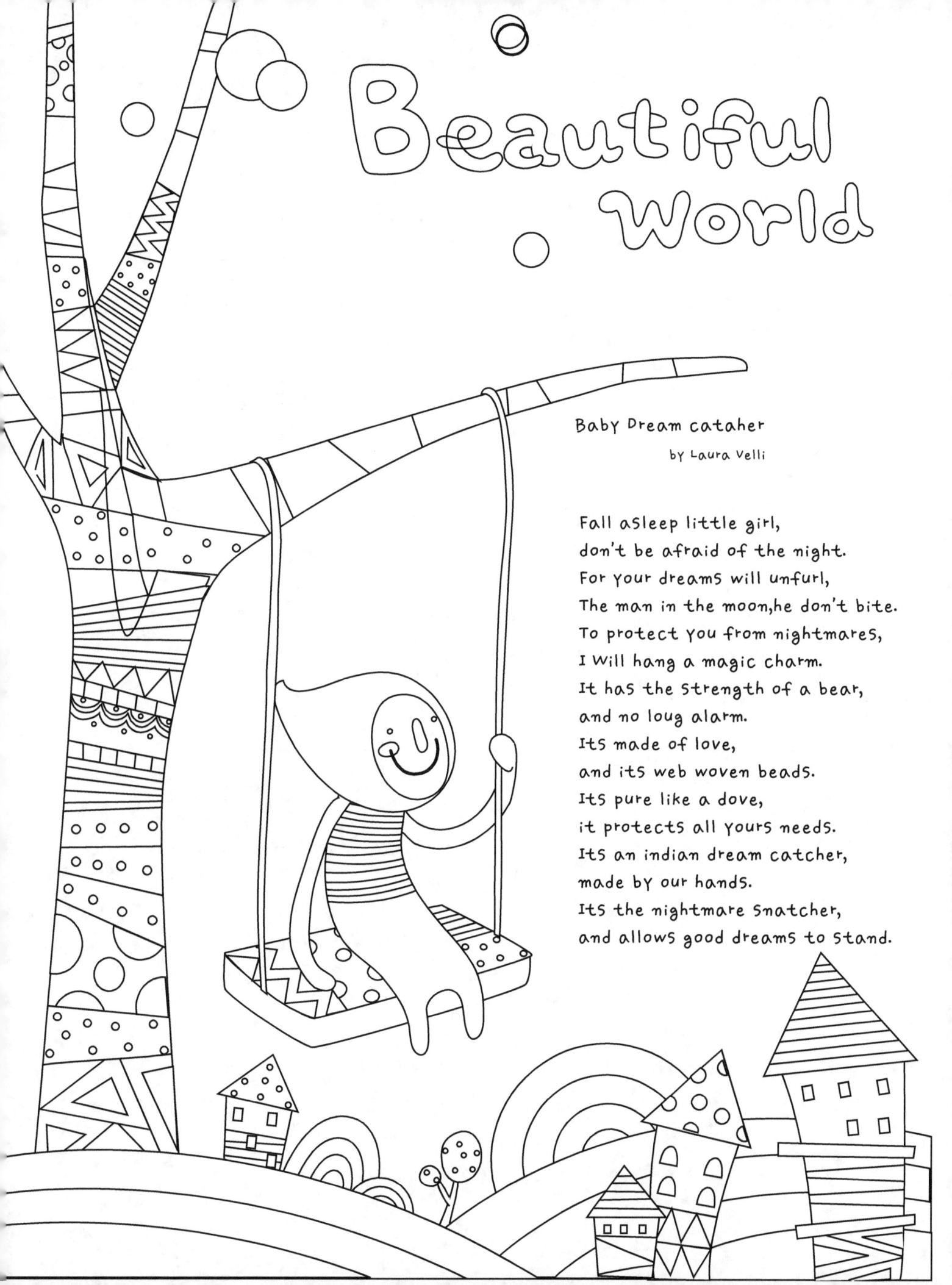

Baby Dream cataher
by Laura Velli

Fall asleep little girl,
don't be afraid of the night.
For your dreams will unfurl,
The man in the moon,he don't bite.
To protect you from nightmares,
I will hang a magic charm.
It has the strength of a bear,
and no loug alarm.
Its made of love,
and its web woven beads.
Its pure like a dove,
it protects all yours needs.
Its an indian dream catcher,
made by our hands.
Its the nightmare Snatcher,
and allows good dreams to stand.

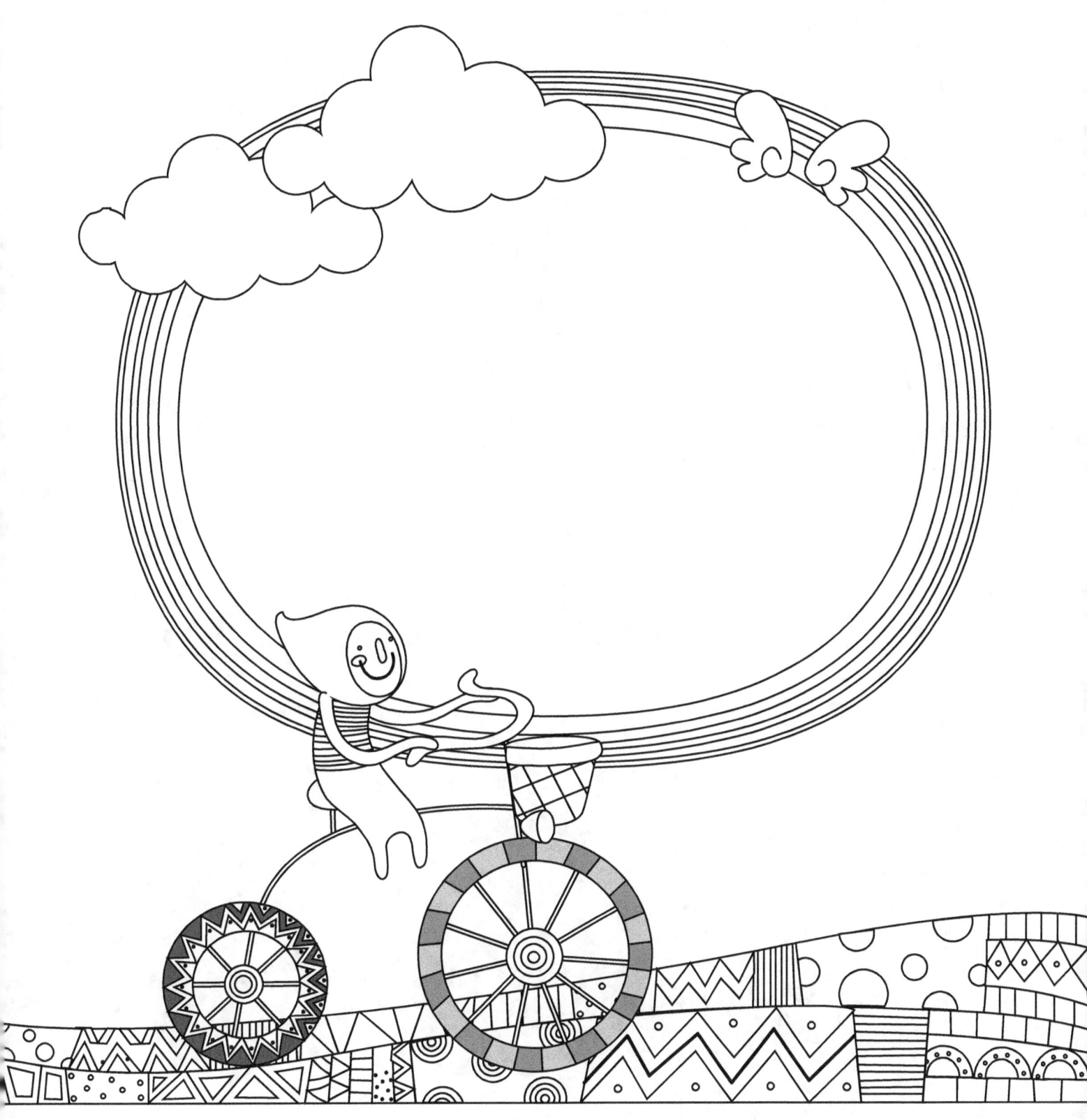

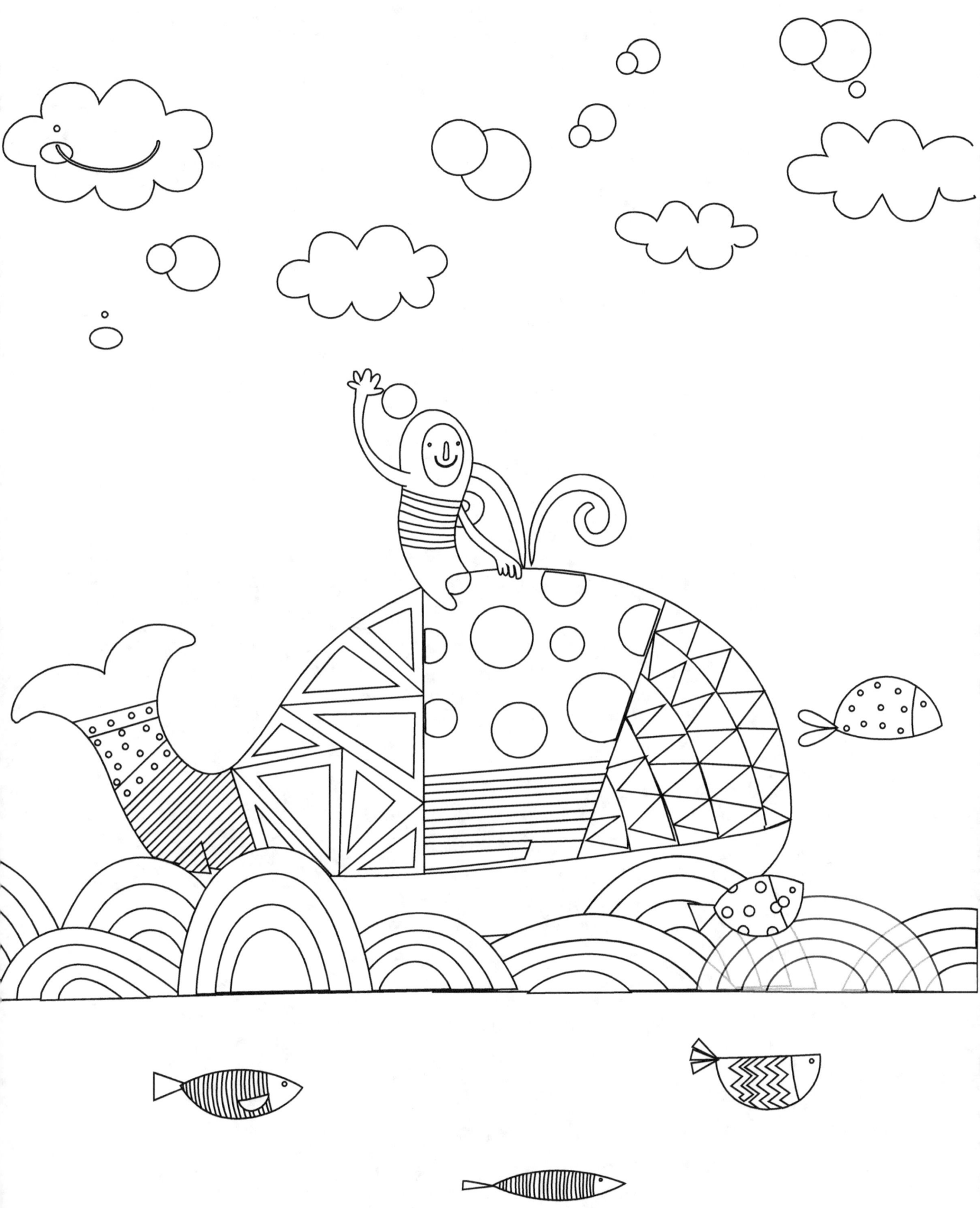

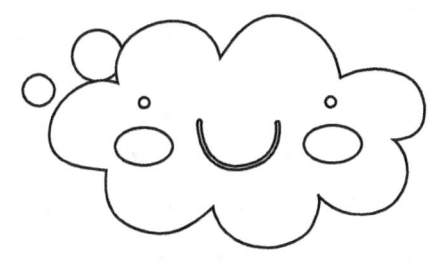

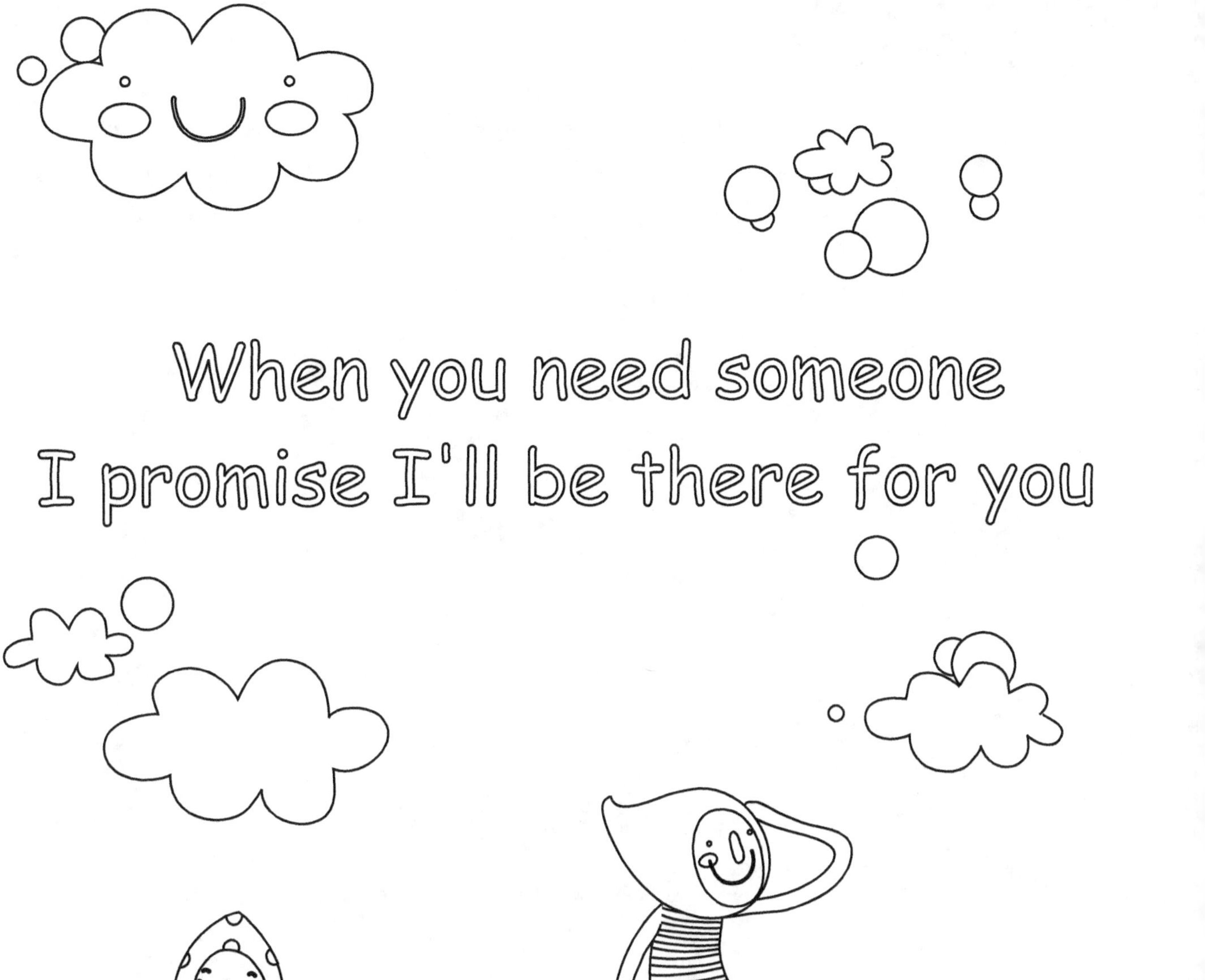

When you need someone
I promise I'll be there for you

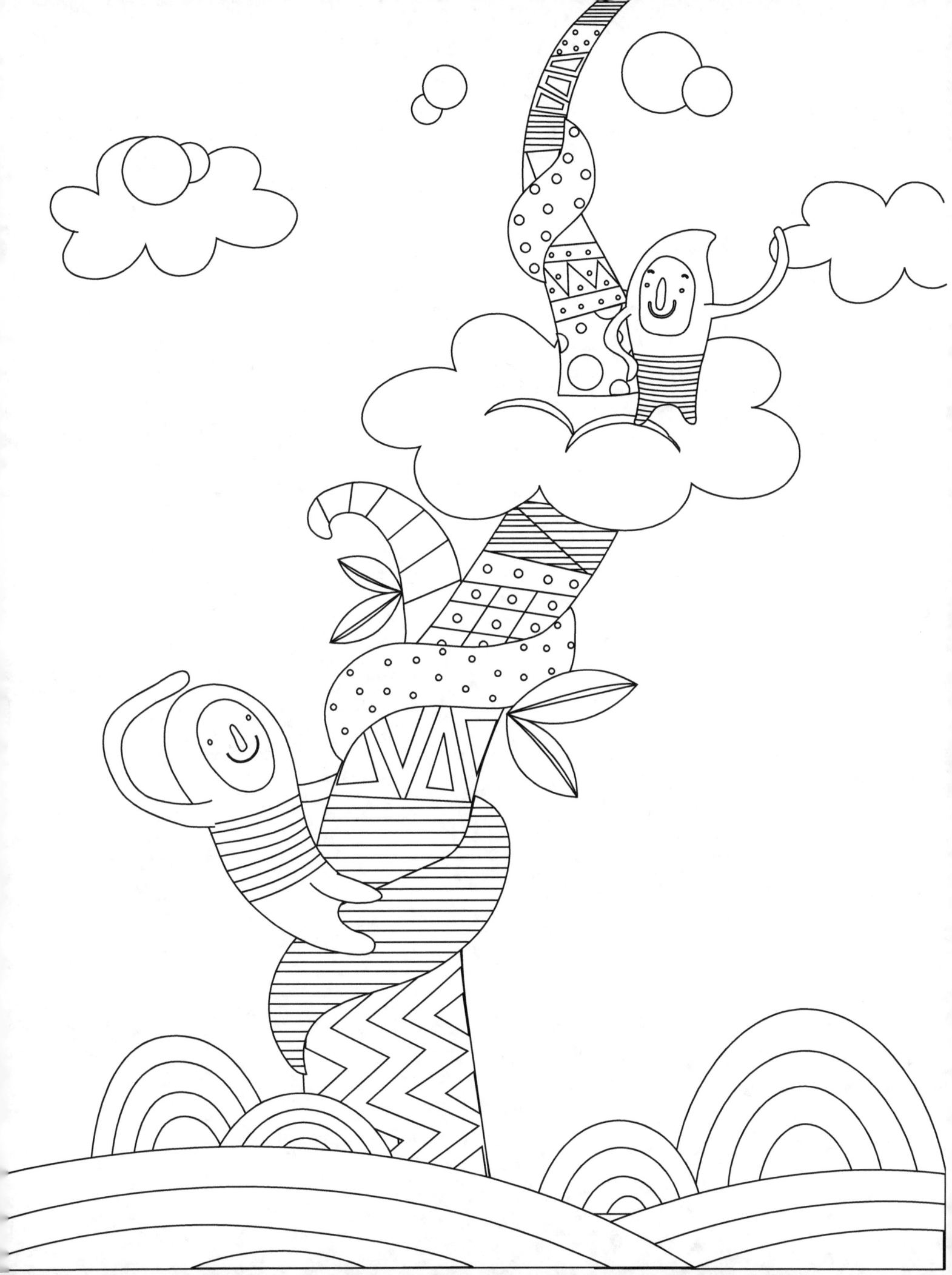

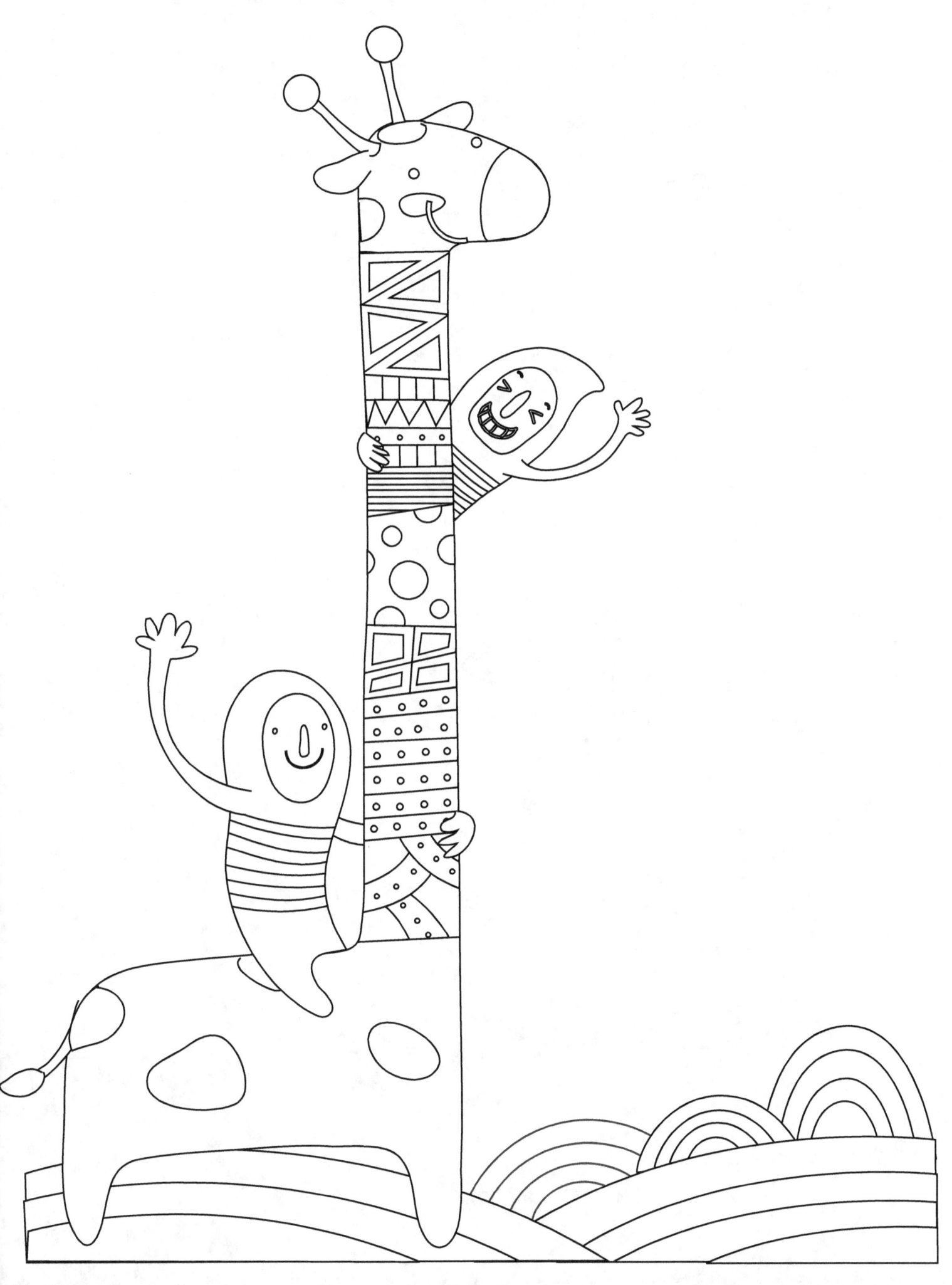

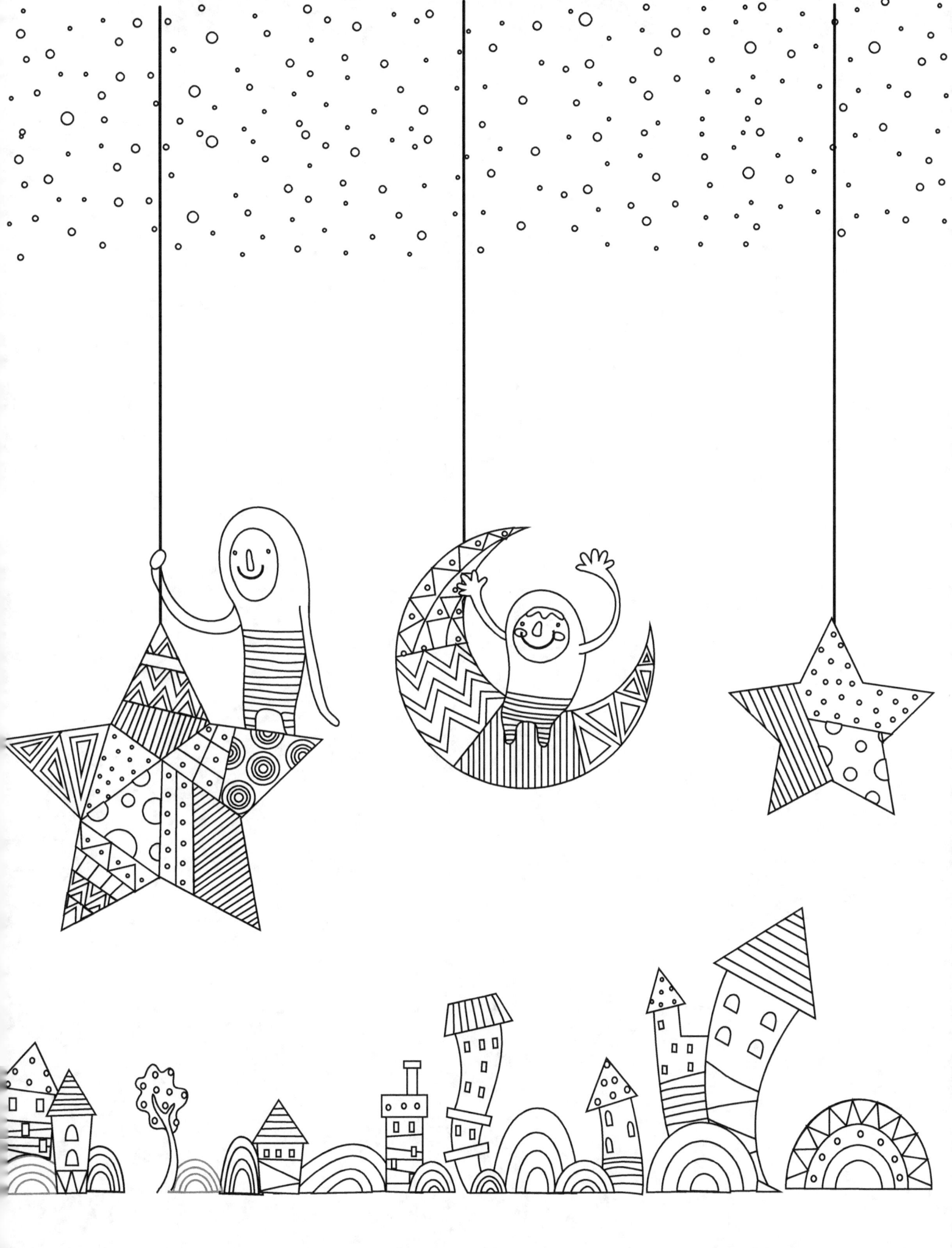

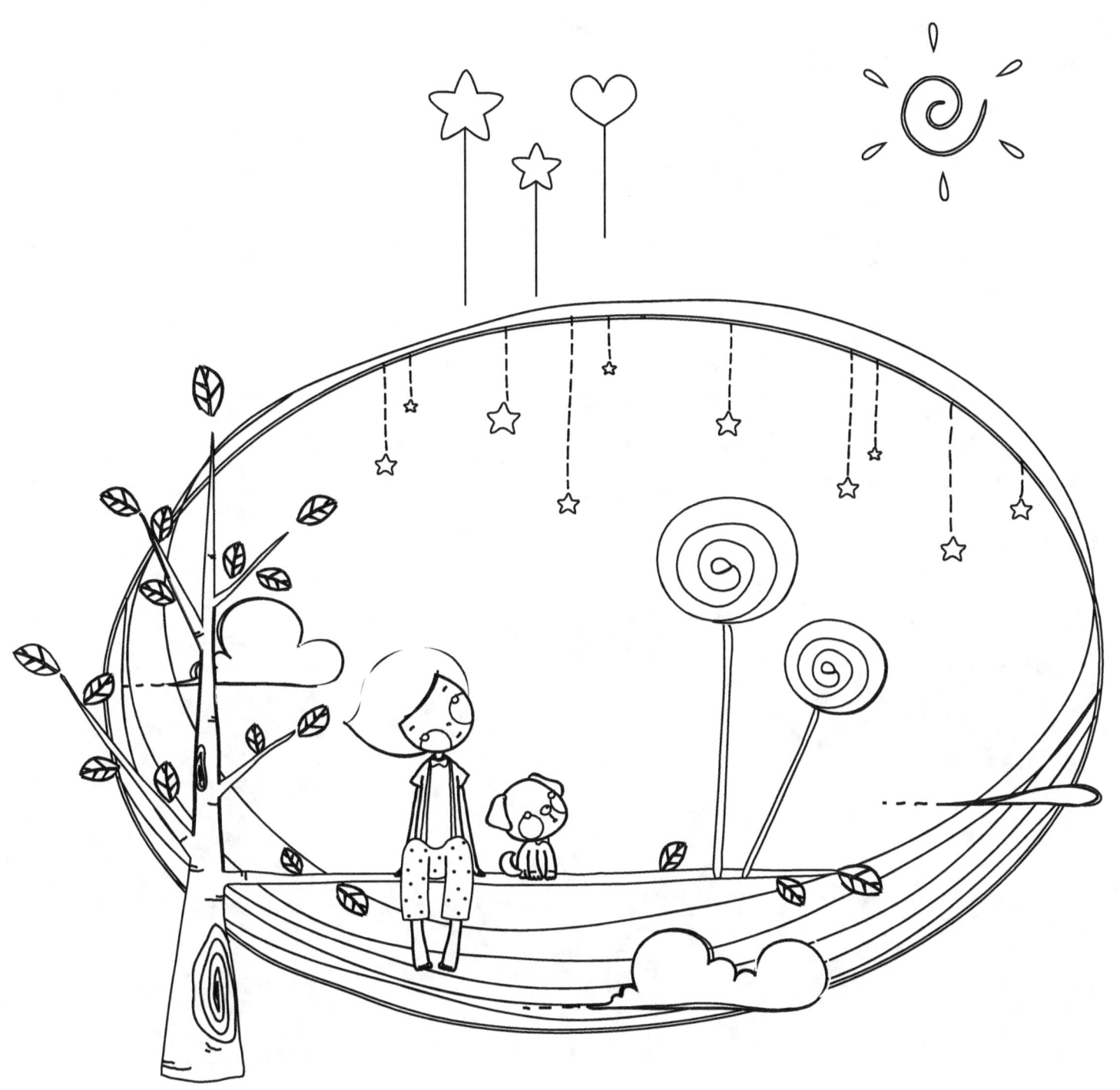

Small and white, Clean and bright,
You look happy to meet me.

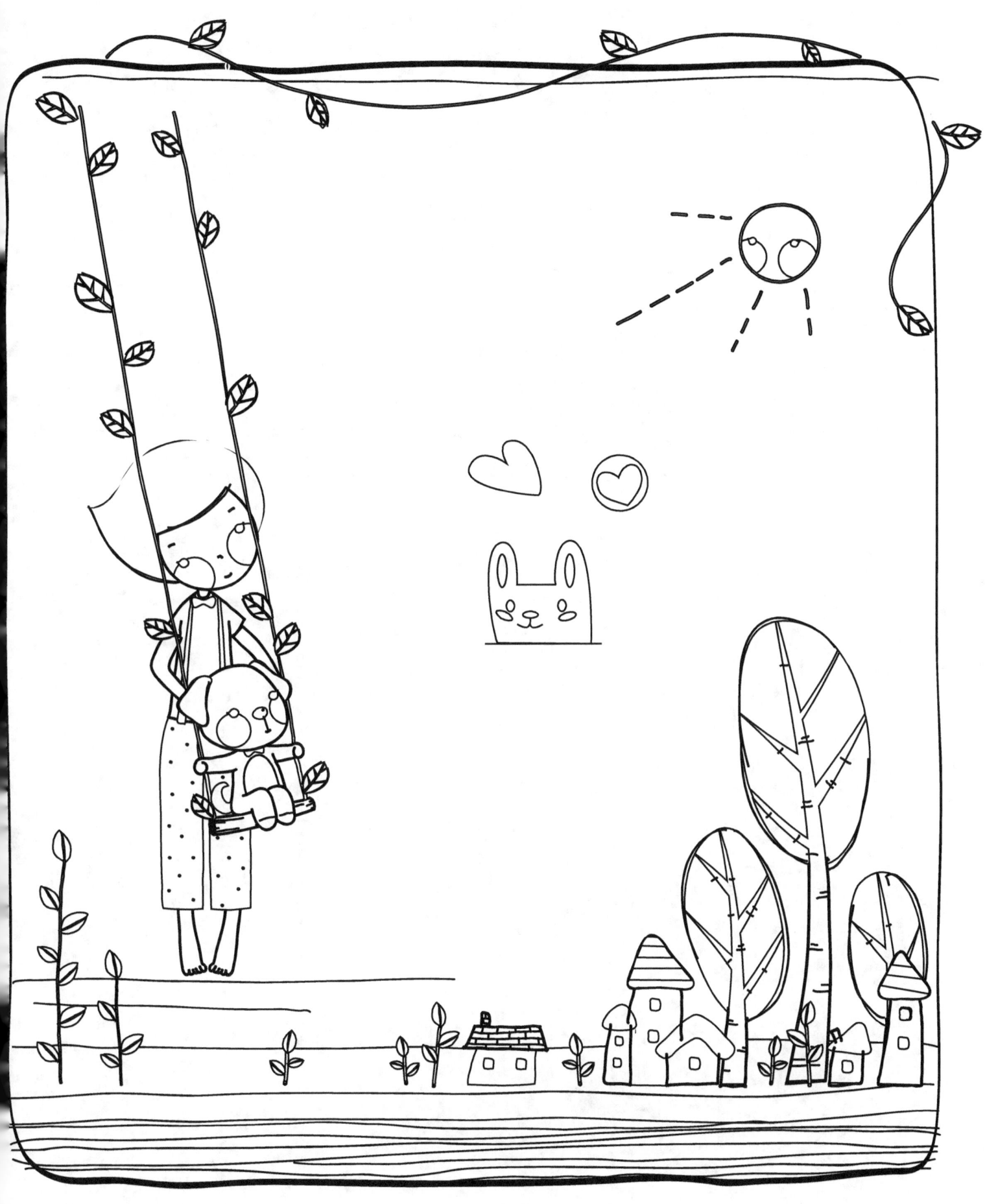

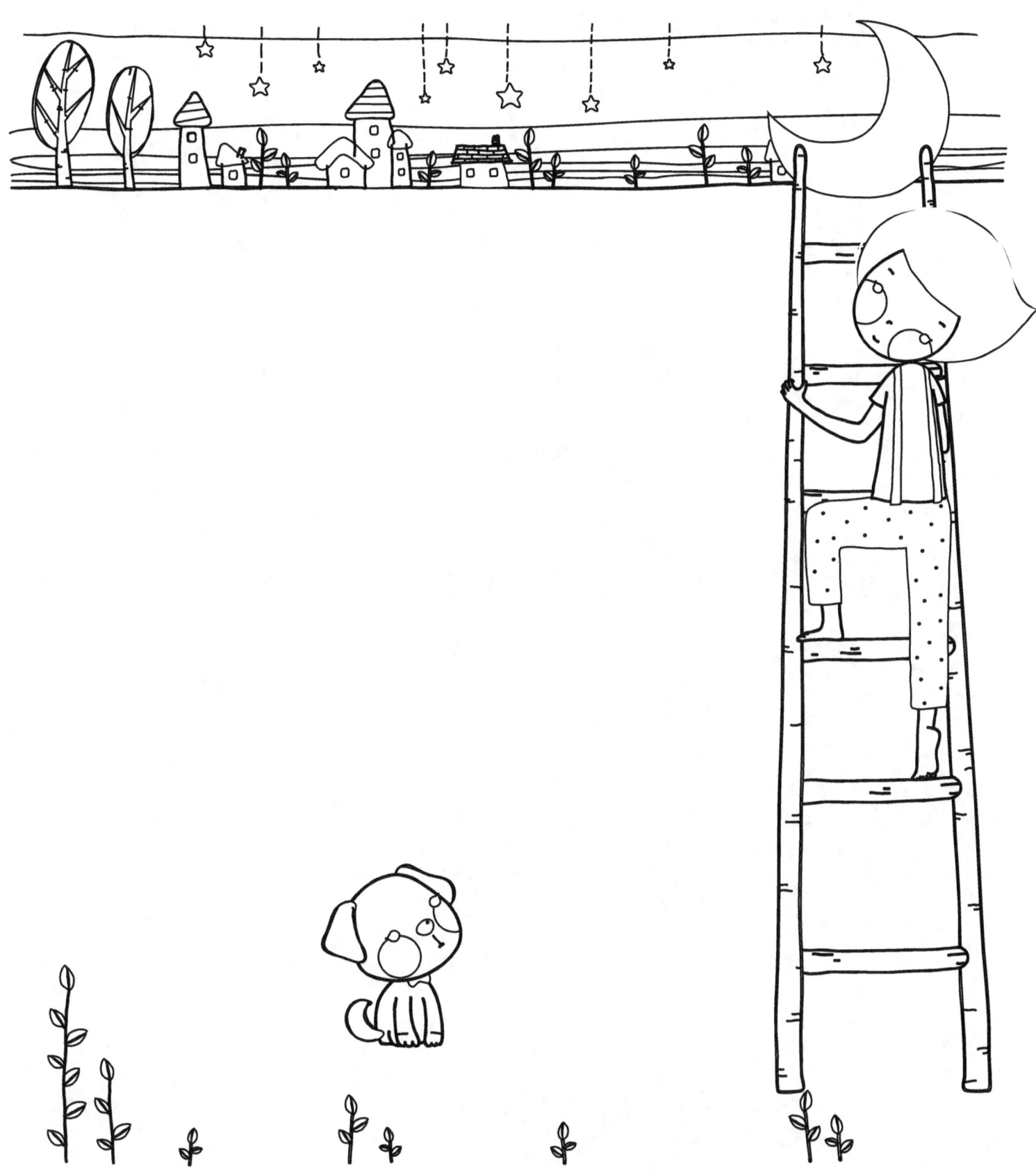

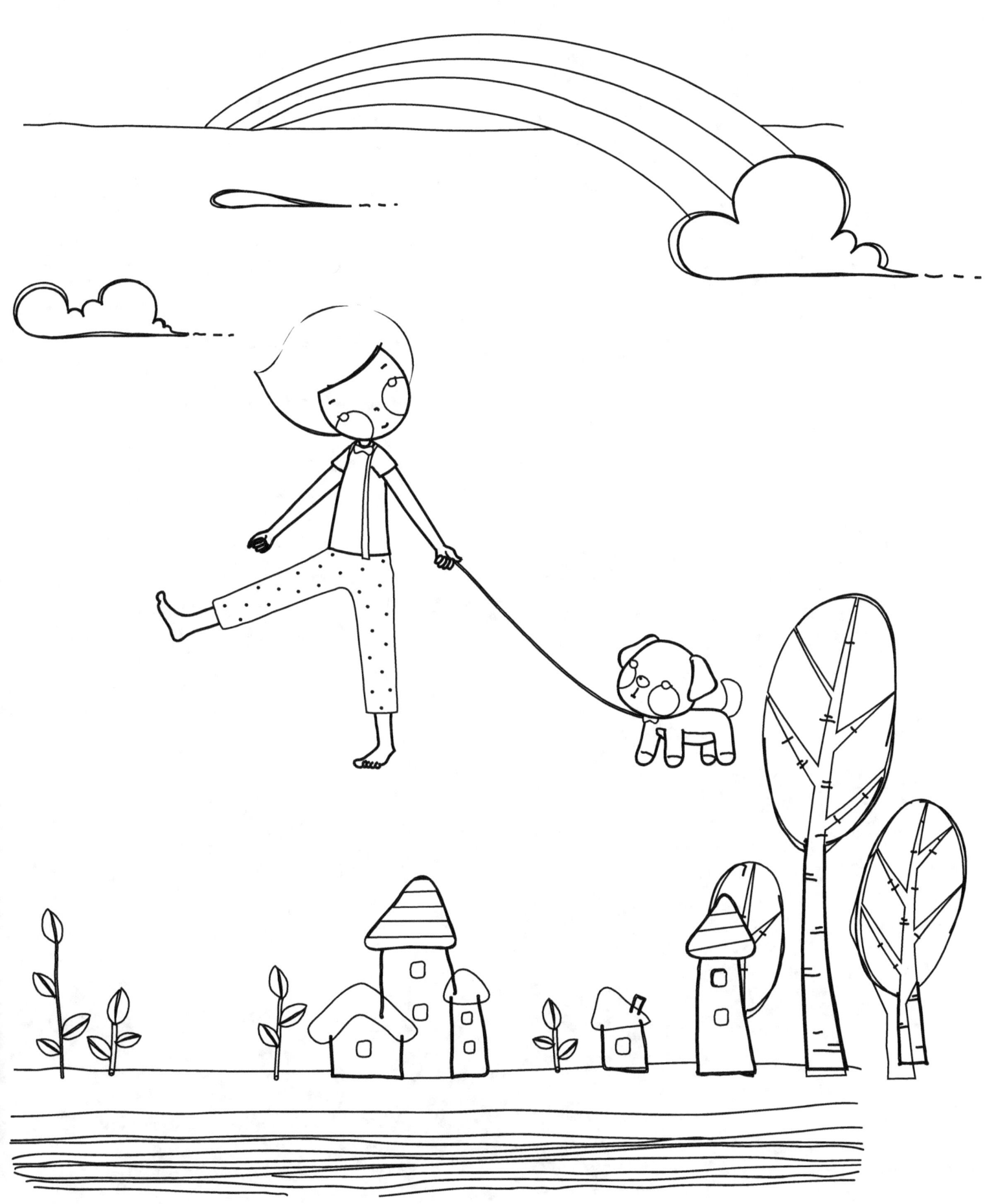

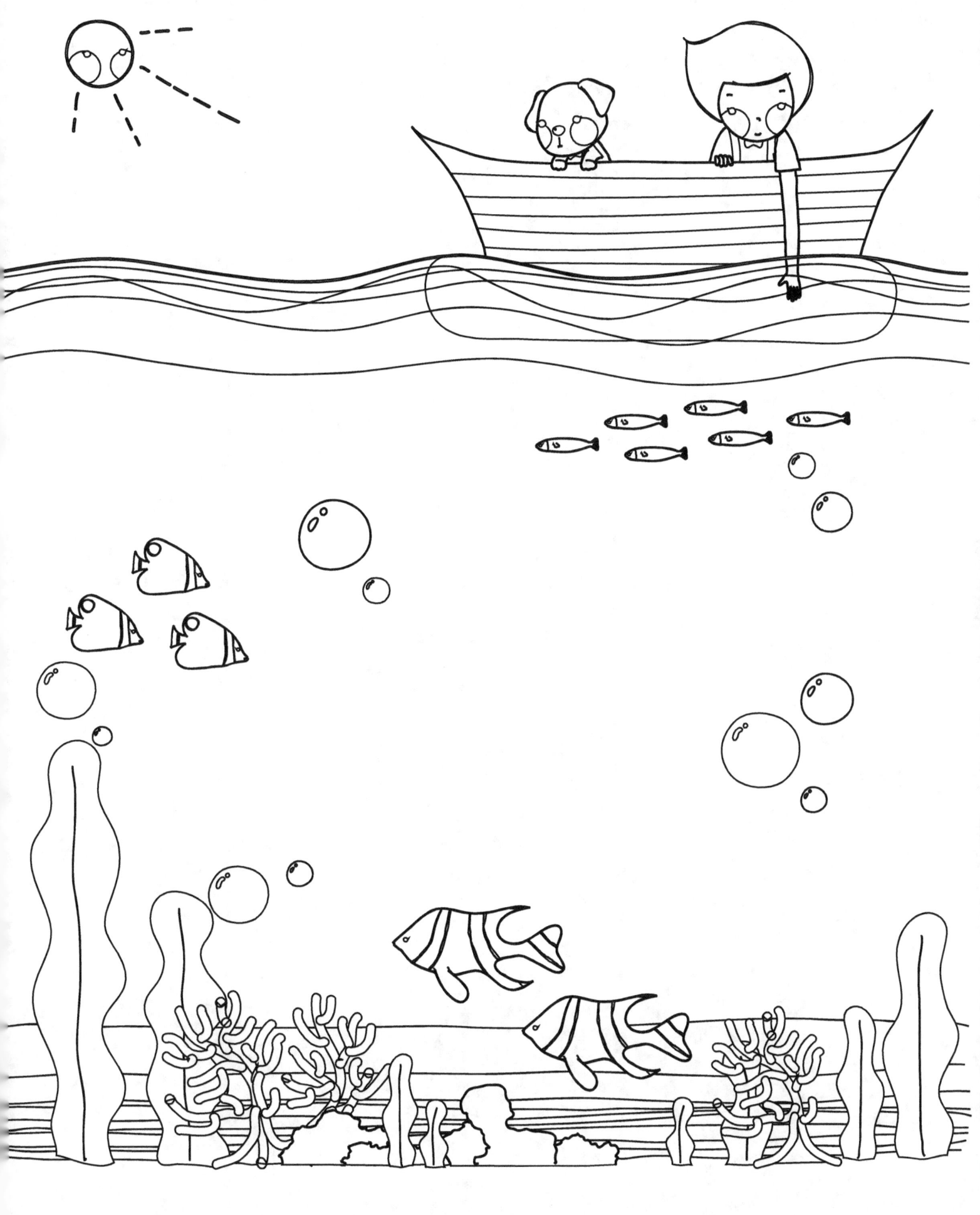

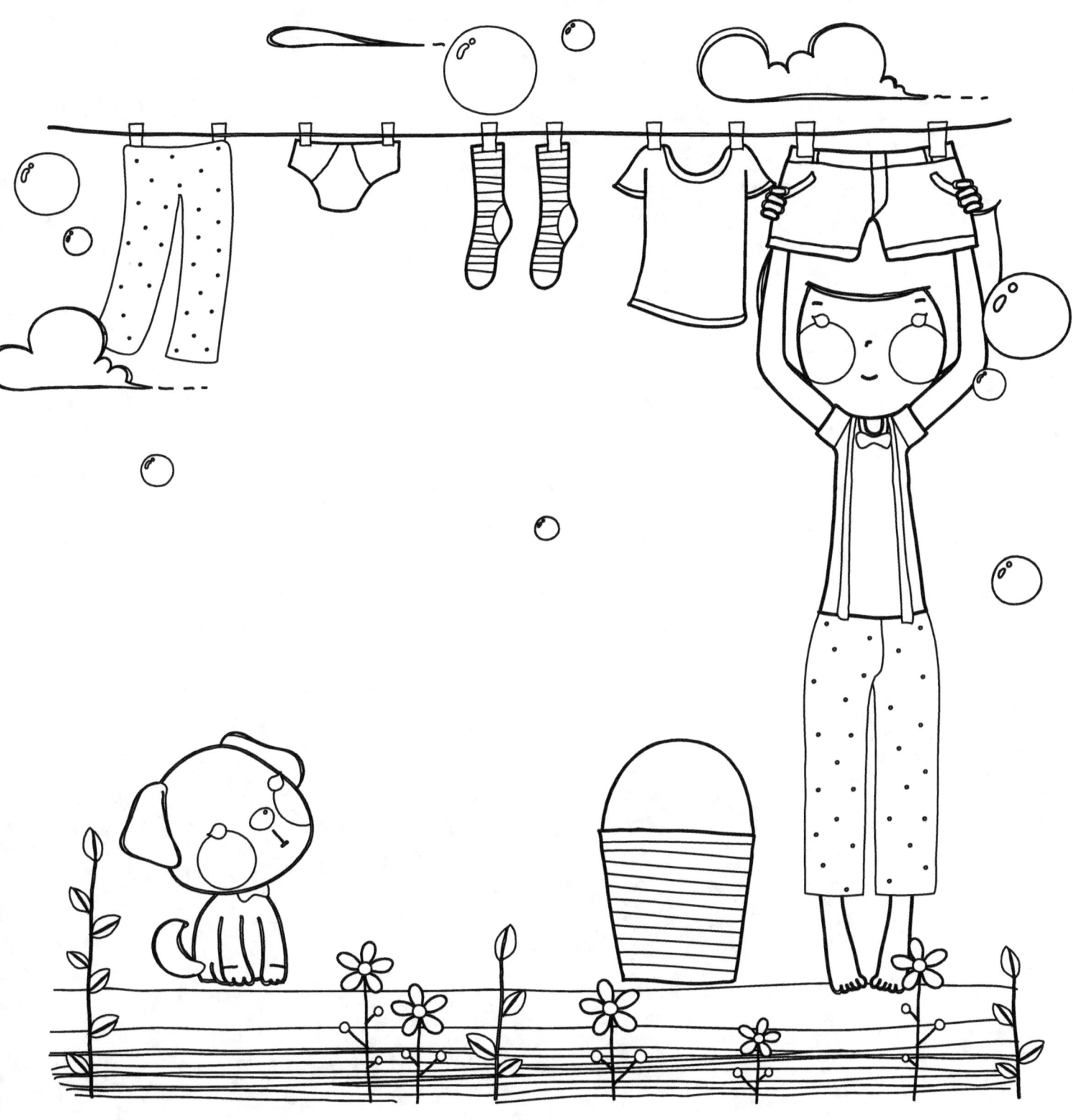

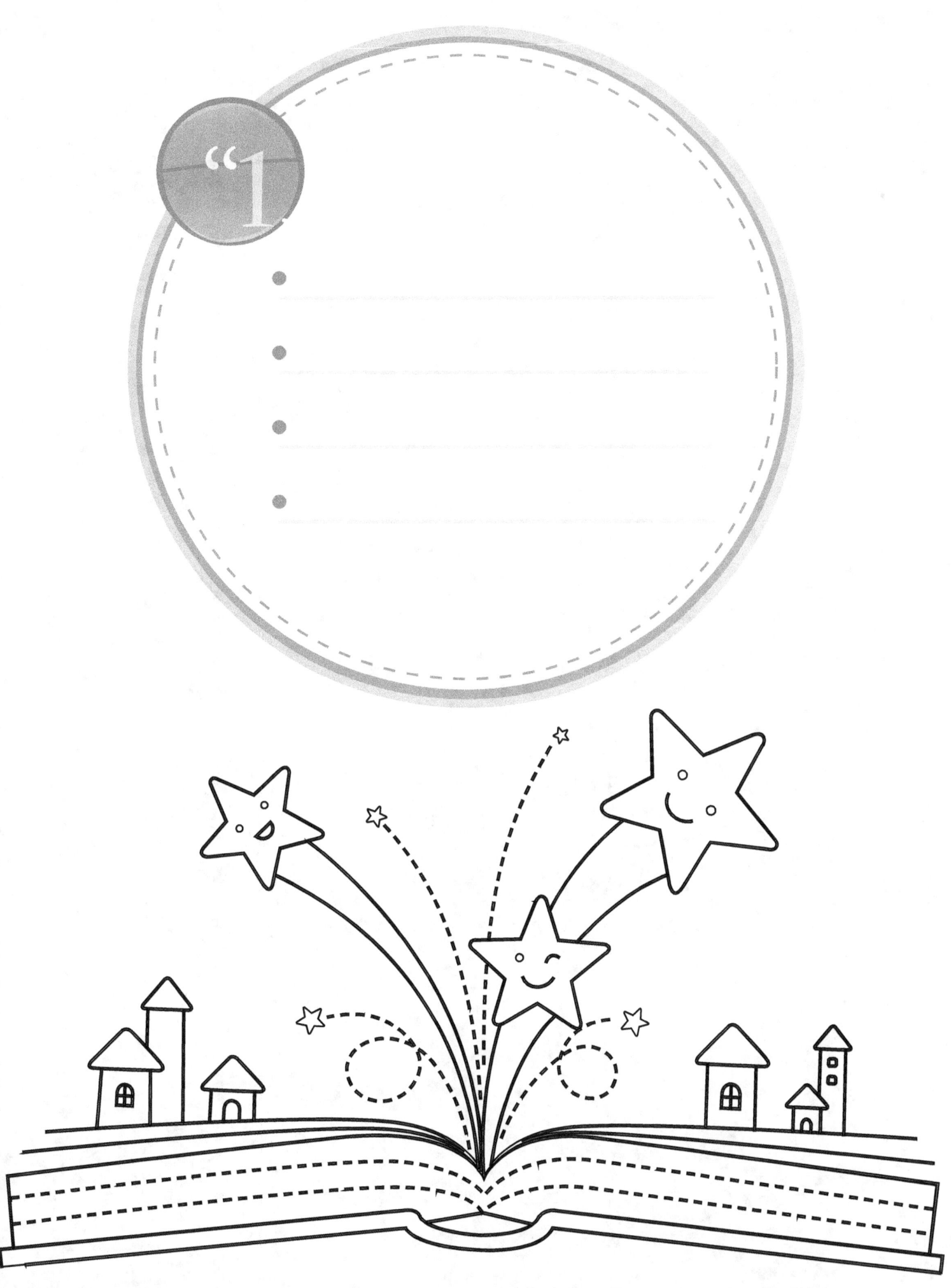

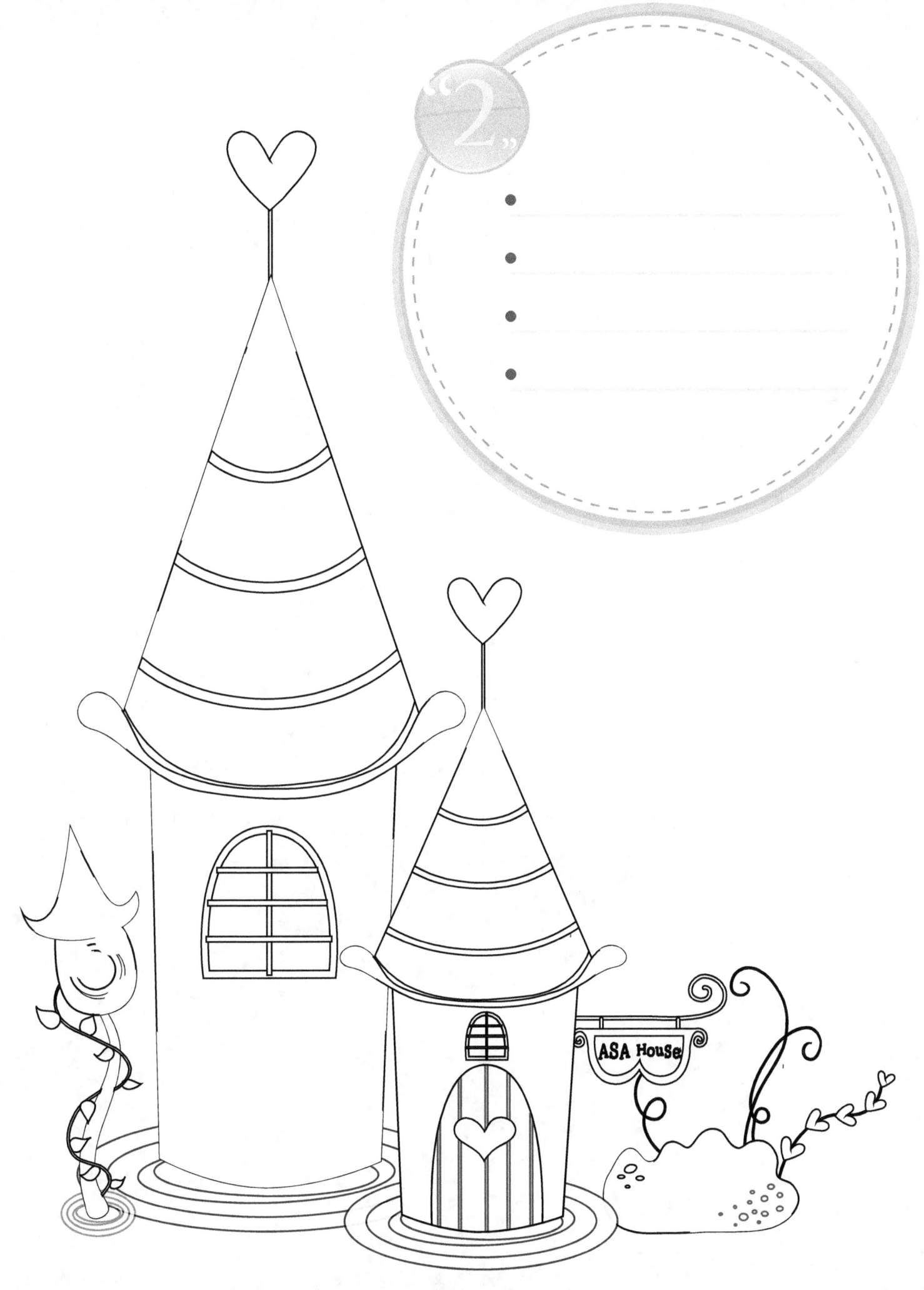

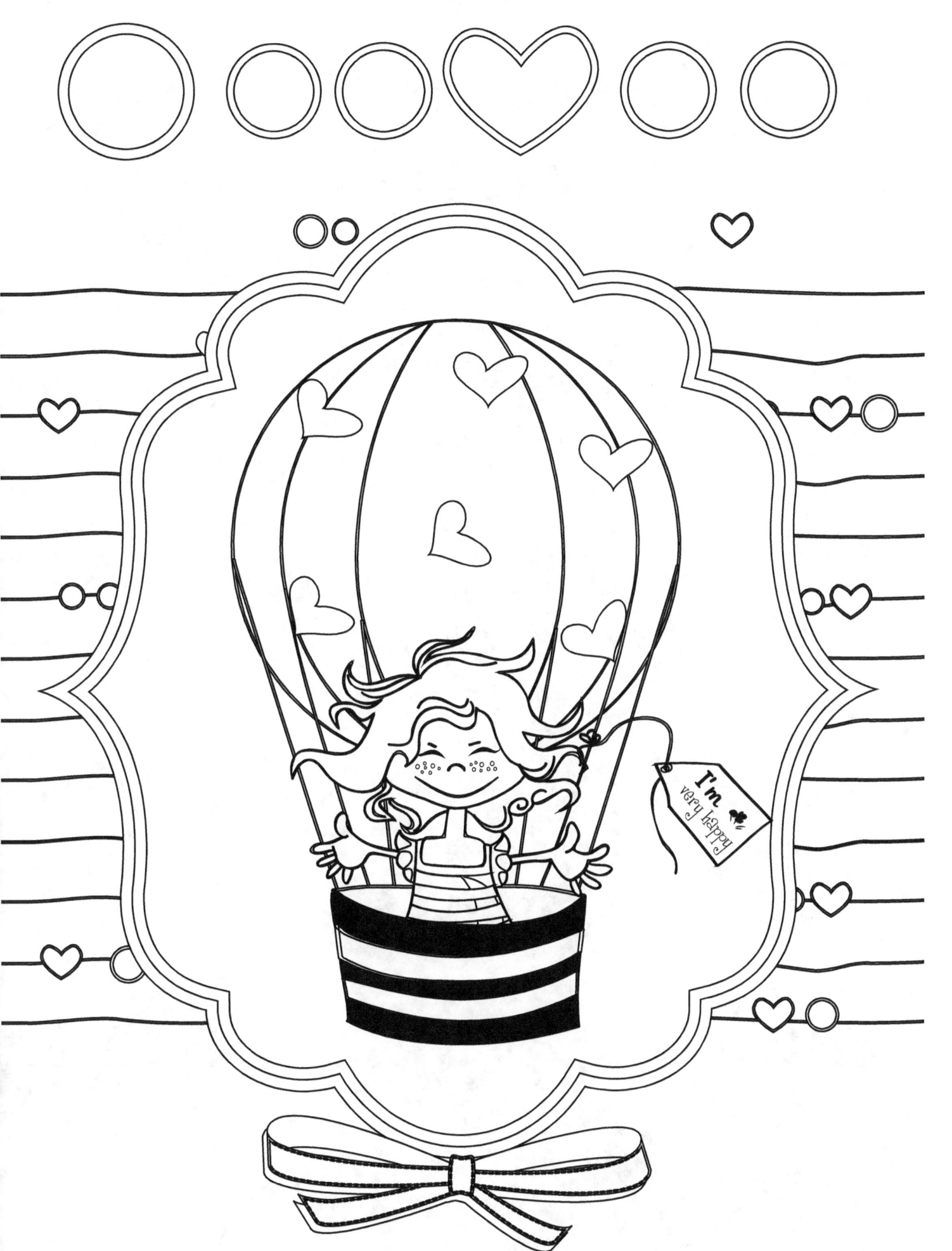

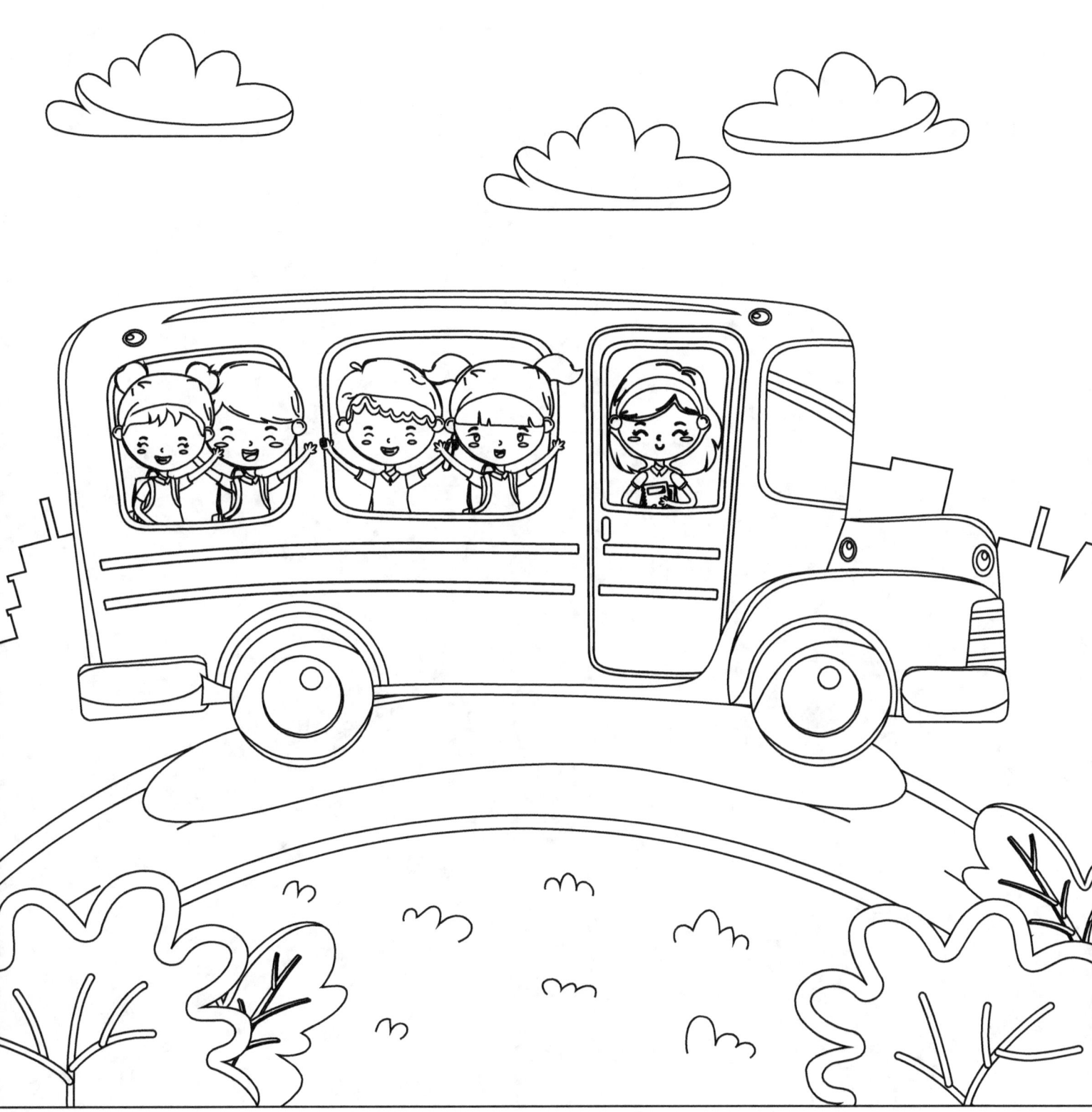

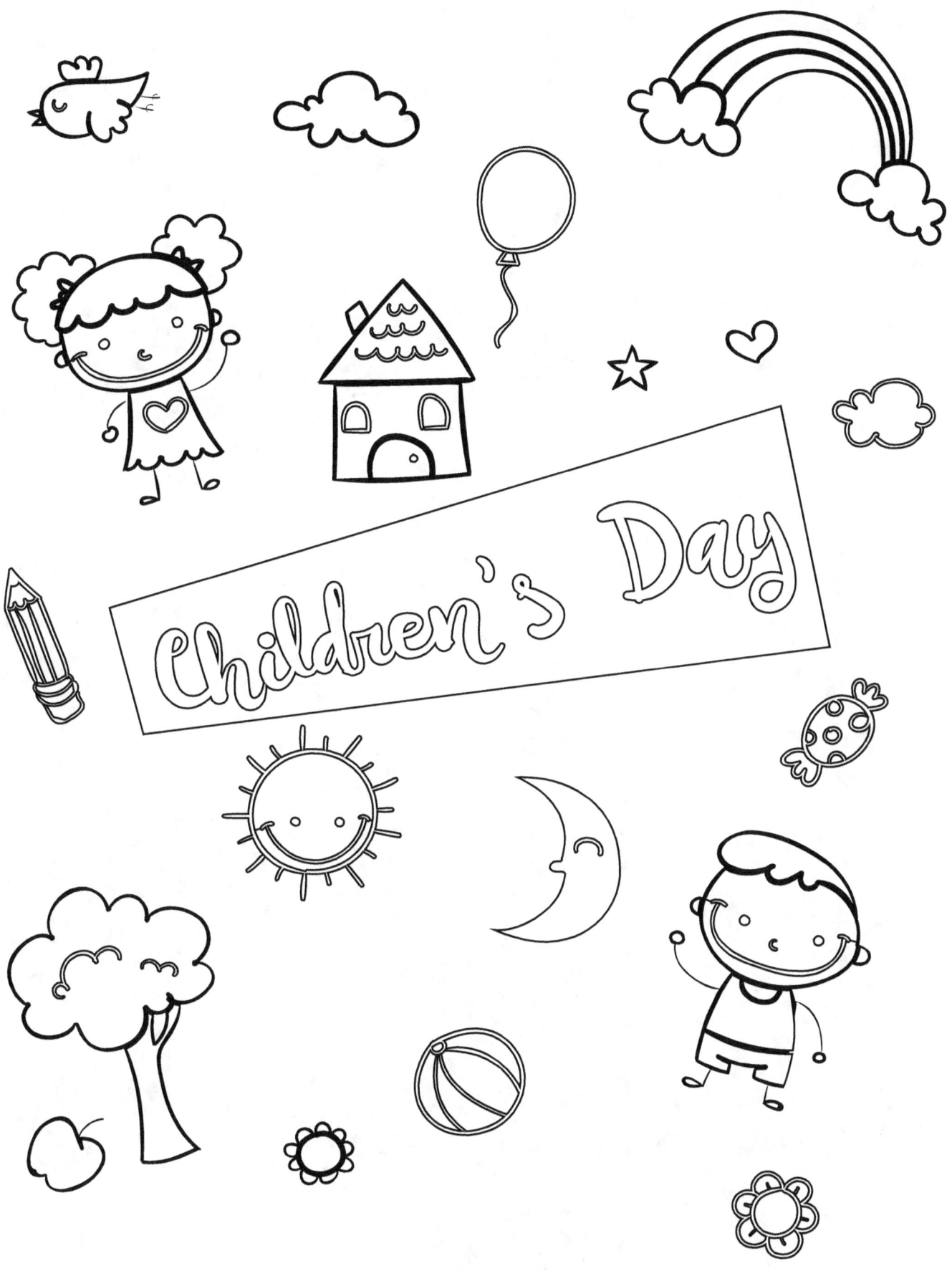

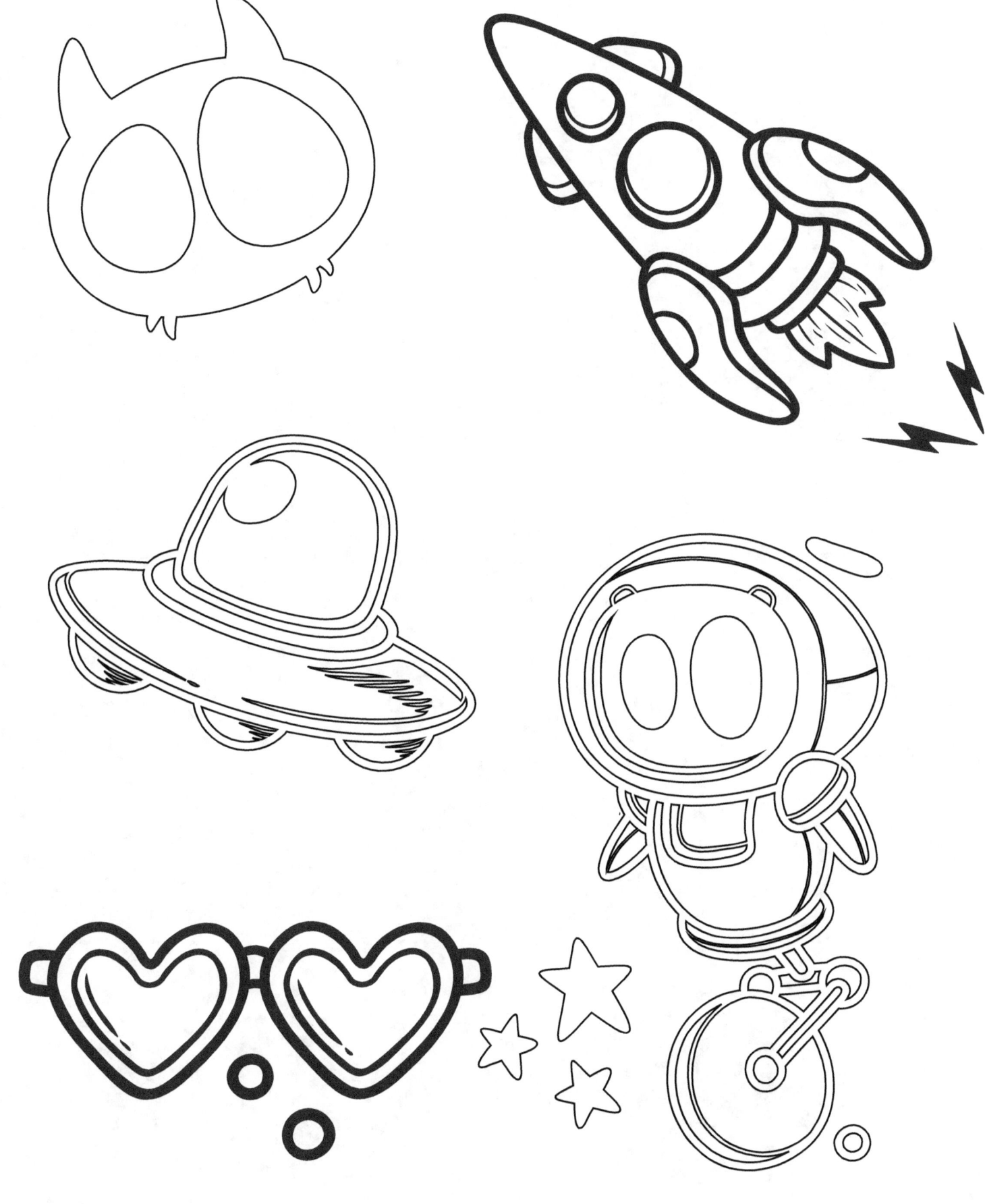

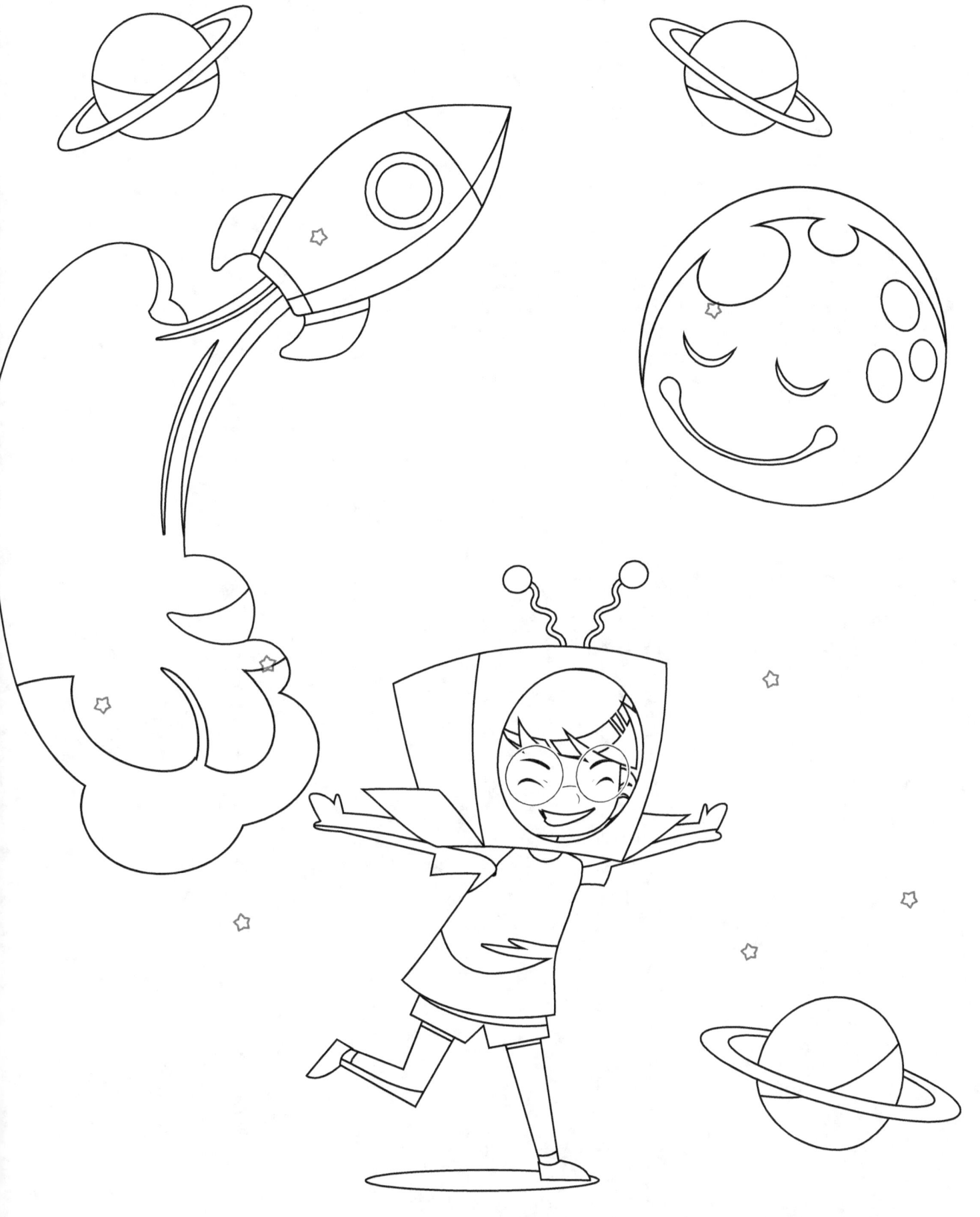

Christmas Toy

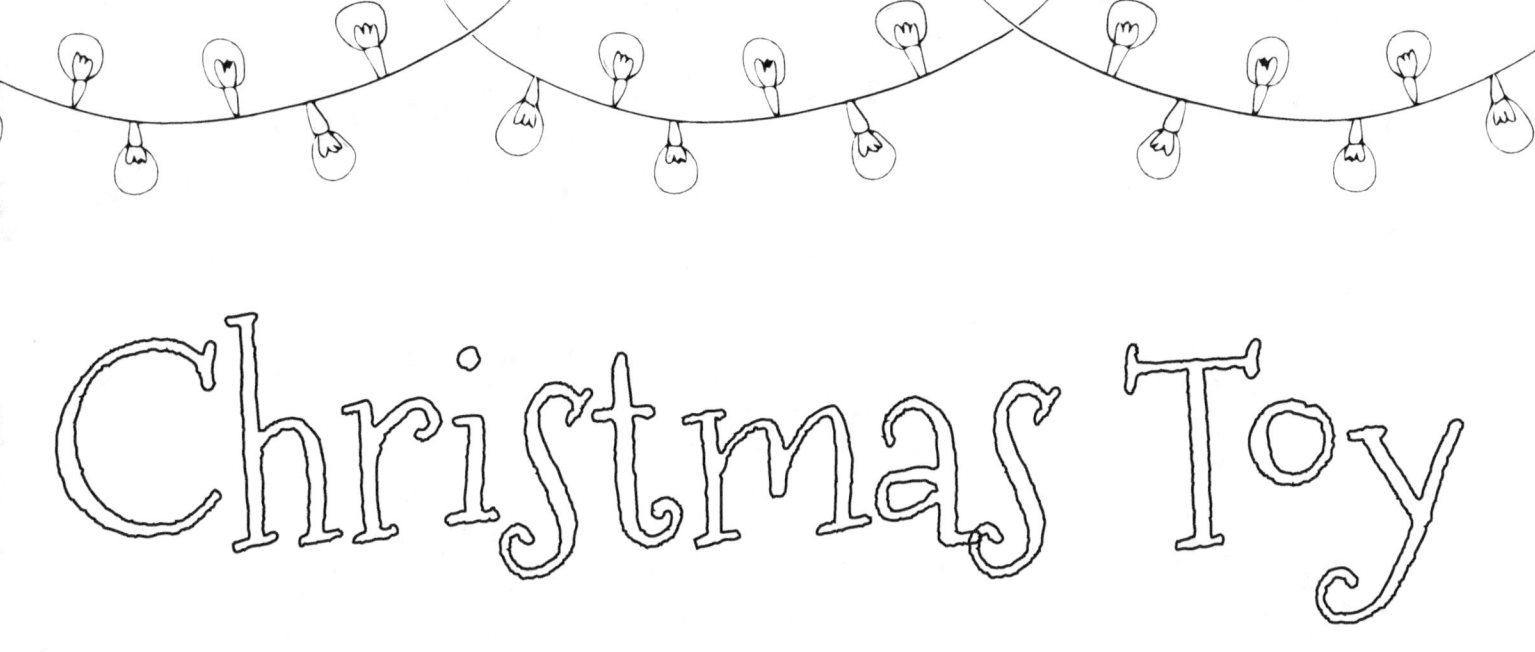

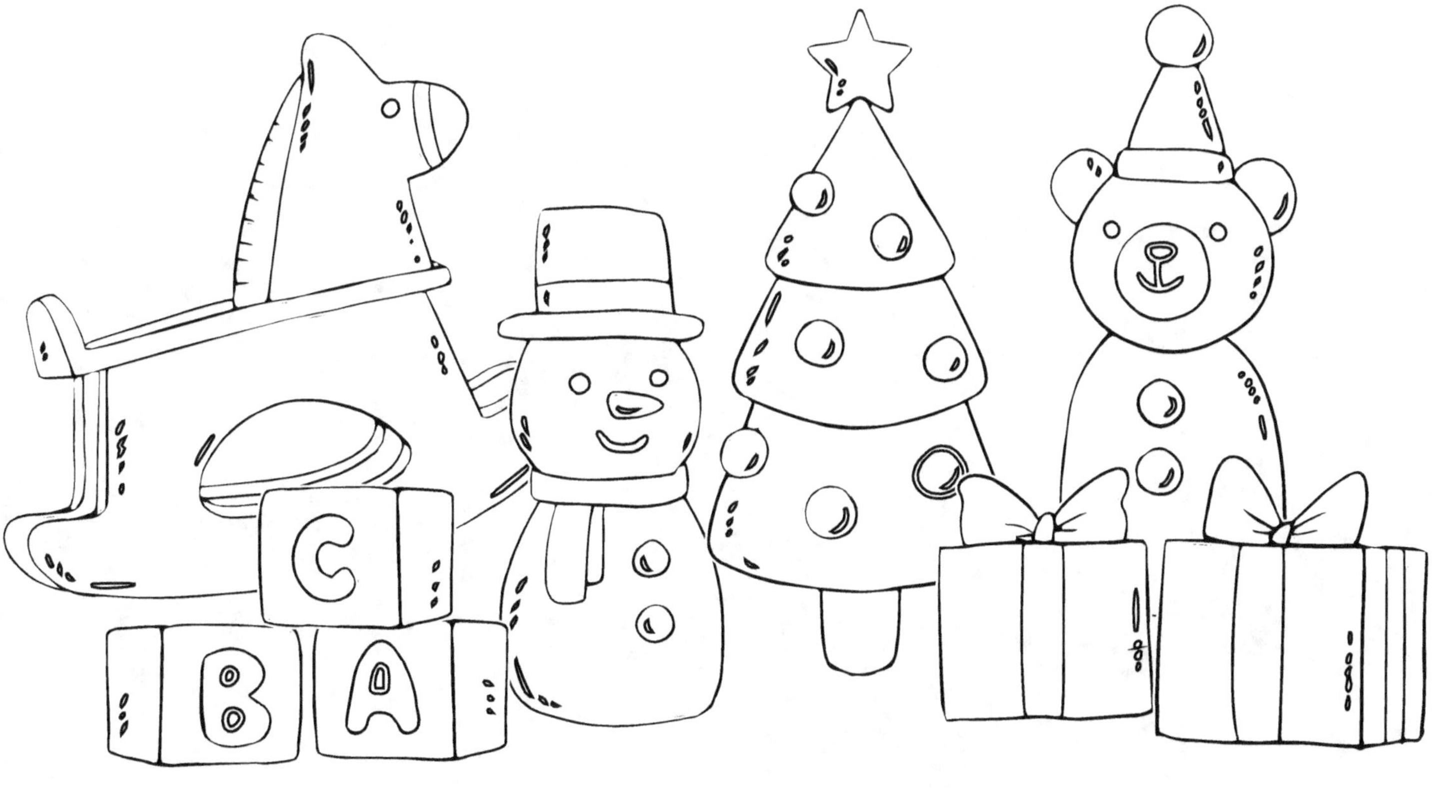

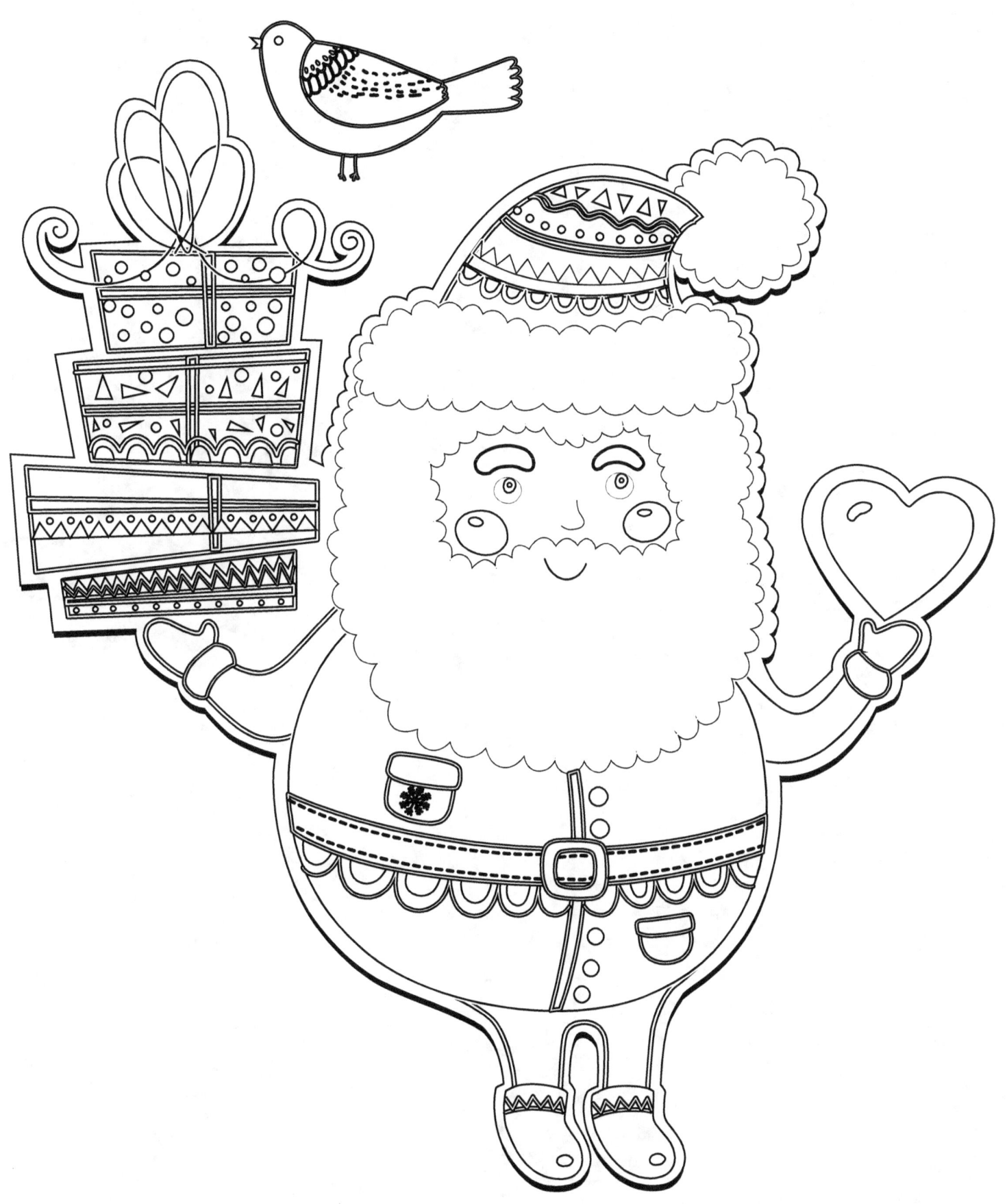

www.ingramcontent.com/pod-product-compliance
Lightning Source LLC
Chambersburg PA
CBHW081529220526
45467CB00010B/3103